THE WORLD OF THE
ANCIENT INCAS

THE WORLD OF THE
ANCIENT INCAS

The extraordinary history of the hidden civilizations of the first peoples
of the South American Andes, with over 200 photographs and illustrations

DR DAVID M JONES

southwater

This edition is published by Southwater
An imprint of Anness Publishing Ltd, Blaby Road, Wigston,
Leicestershire LE18 4SE

info@anness.com

www.southwaterbooks.com; www.annesspublishing.com

Anness Publishing has a new picture agency outlet for images
for publishing, promotions or advertising. Please visit our
website www.practicalpictures.com for more information.

Publisher: Joanna Lorenz
Editor: Joy Wotton
Designer: Nigel Partridge
Illustrations and maps: Vanessa Card and Anthony Duke
Production Controller: Christine Ni

ETHICAL TRADING POLICY
Because of our ongoing ecological investment programme, you,
as our customer, can have the pleasure and reassurance of knowing that a tree is being cultivated on your behalf to naturally
replace the materials used to make the book you are holding. For
further information about this scheme, go to www.annesspub-
lishing.com/trees

Previously published as part of a larger volume *The Inca World*

PUBLISHER'S NOTE
Although the information in this book is believed to be
accurate and true at the time of going to press, neither the
authors nor the publisher can accept any legal responsibility or
liability for any errors or omissions that may have been made
nor for any inaccuracies nor for any loss, harm or injury that
comes about from following information in this book.

*p.1 Rope bridge, Poma de Ayala, c. 1615. p.2 The Ponce Monolith,
Tiwanaku. p.3 Machu Picchu. Below: Farming, Poma de
Ayala, c. 1615.*

CONTENTS

INTRODUCTION

The Inca Empire was the culmination of thousands of years of cultural evolution, the end product of gradual developments from small farming villages to cities with large populations and sophisticated political, economic and religious organization.

THE SOURCES

Scholars have three information sources about the Incas and their predecessors: historical documents, archaeological evidence, and anthropological or ethnological information about Andean peoples.

Written sources are particularly relevant for our picture of Inca society, but the principal sources of knowledge for pre-Inca civilization come from archaeology and anthropology. Artefacts and structures are direct evidence of what ancient Andeans made and used. But the manner of their use and what social, political, economic and religious meanings they have must be interpreted.

For pre-Inca cultures there is almost no historical evidence. Inca records of the peoples they conquered (for example the Chimú Kingdom that began before the Inca Empire and was contemporary to the early Inca), written down after the

Below: Andean foothills, typical upland valley terrain and Mount Illimani, Bolivia.

Spanish Conquest, are subject to Inca imperial views. However, comparison of pre-Inca archaeological evidence with Inca materials and history can reveal similarities that enable scholars to suggest that Inca social, political, economic and religious practices and beliefs were the end results of much earlier developments of these themes.

ARCHAEOLOGICAL PROJECTIONS

In combination with archaeology, much of what we gain from written sources about the Incas and their contemporaries can be 'projected' into the past, as a way of interpreting and understanding pre-Inca civilization and cultures.

Archaeology comprises methods of recovery, analytical procedures and reasoning to reconstruct as much as possible about the nature of people's lives in past cultures. Archaeological evidence is viable wherever and whenever historical evidence does not exist, or does not document groups or aspects of a people or culture. In addition to excavating and collecting artefacts (any object or remains made by humans or left as the result of their activities), archaeologists carefully record their contexts – the positions and relationships between artefacts and the soil in which they are found.

Above: Inca maize planting in August (yupuy quilla, soil turning) depicted in Poma de Ayala's Nueva Corónica, c.1615.

DATING

Historical sources normally give dates for the events being recorded, although these are not always accurate. Until 1949 archaeological evidence, unless it could be linked to a historical source, could not be given calendar dates, only dates relative to other archaeological evidence (before, after or at the same time as). Such relative dating was determined by association in the same stratigraphic layer of earth, or in a layer above (later than) or below (earlier than) another artefact. This is true whether the artefact concerned is something small, such as a hand tool, or large, such as the foundation walls of a temple.

Science has discovered several radiometric ways to determine absolute dates for archaeological materials. Two principal methods are radiocarbon dating and dendrochronology (tree-ring dating). The former is the main method for Andean ancient history because its limits (back to about 50,000 years ago) are well within the range of human occupation of the Andean Area. The latter was developed

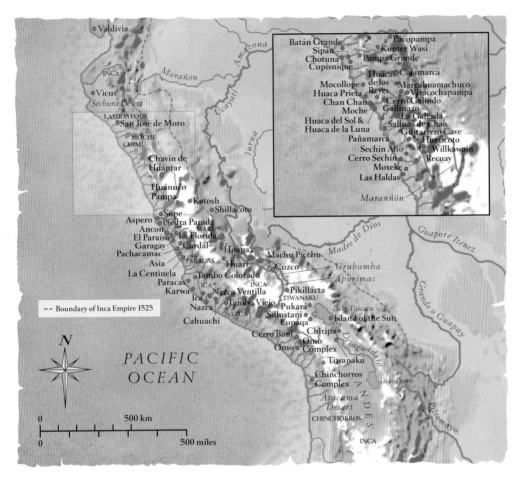

Above: Map of the Andean Area, showing sites, of all periods, discussed in the text.

from the early decades of the 20th century but is of no use in Andean cultures because most of the wood used in Andean architecture has not survived, and a tree-ring sequence is not available for the region.

CAUTION

Archaeological evidence has drawbacks. Many human activities produce no physical objects or traces. For example, languages, religious beliefs or social relationships usually leave no direct remains and can only be deduced from related artefacts (e.g. written sources, idols in a temple, burial practices or the nature of house plans). Many organic materials are destroyed by natural decay (such as wood, fibre, bones and plant materials), although some natural conditions (extreme dryness, burning or lack of air) sometimes preserve organic materials. Humans themselves often destroy their own artefacts through use, abandonment or war.

ANTHROPOLOGY

Ethnological information about contemporary Andean people can provide insight into ancient cultures. Because the landscape in remote Andean regions has changed little since Inca times, some ancient traditions and technology have survived, particularly agricultural methods. Observations of contemporary society can help in the interpretation of otherwise puzzling archaeological remains or historical descriptions, through direct parallels or as models for comparison. One of the major characteristics of Andean civilization appears to be longevity of technology, cultural practices, social organization and religious belief, which are recognizably different in detail to distinguish diverse peoples and nations through time.

The direct observations of Felipe Guaman Poma de Ayala and the sources used by Bernabé Cobo were the first ethnographies. Later explorers and travellers added to and confirmed many 16th-century records when they recorded native practices. Joining a French expedition to South America in the late 1730s, Antonio Juan de Ulloa recorded contemporary Andean practices.

Later, Alexander von Humboldt travelled throughout the Americas and recorded his observations on natural history and geology, ethnology and archaeology. His *Political Essay on the Kingdom of New Spain* (1811) and *Researches Concerning the Institutions and Monuments of the Ancient Inhabitants of America* (1814) were monumental works, and his lectures back in Europe brought South America and its peoples into public awareness.

Below: Highland plateau among the Cordillera de los Frailes, Bolivia.

DISCOVERING THE INCAS AND THEIR PREDECESSORS

Awareness of ancient civilizations in the New World began to increase in the late 18th and 19th centuries as excavations and the collecting of antiquities developed. Primitive excavations were undertaken in Europe and the Americas. Scholars began to re-examine colonial records, old maps and the objects taken back to Europe by the conquistadors and surviving in ancient graves. Sadly, then and now, the antiquities black market encourages looting, and the ancient sites of South America are riddled with *huaqueros'* (tomb robbers') pits.

The archaeologists and anthropologists of the time began to ask serious questions about the past, and when the ancient historians failed them, or, in the New World, simply did not exist, they began to use archaeology and ethnology to seek their own answers. Their early efforts went little beyond recognition, recording and description of ancient objects and sites. Gradually, however, their growing knowledge led to fieldwork designed to answer specific questions about the rise of civilization in the ancient Andes, and to address the 'problem' of the very presence of white people in the New World prior to the arrival of Europeans.

Modern archaeologists and anthropologists developed sophisticated techniques and reasoning during the 20th century to explore Andean civilizations, and continue their quest into the 21st century.

Left: Archaeologists cleaning the base of one of the many temple tombs at Sipán in the Lambayeque Valley, Peru.

NATIVE AND SPANISH SOURCES

Much of European knowledge about native Andeans was biased according to the viewpoint and nationality of the author of any written source. Early sources are mostly limited to information about the Incas, and authors throughout the later 16th and 17th centuries often copied from earlier writers, so reinforcing their views.

NATIVE RECORD-KEEPING

Neither the Incas nor any earlier Andean civilization developed writing. The Incas did, however, invent a system of record keeping called the *quipu*. This was a system of knot tying and colour coding, kept by trained court officials called *quipucamayoqs*. Records were kept as bundles of llama wool threads, suspended from a main thread or rod. The types, colours and sequences of knots, the directions of tying and other details served as tabulations of the numbers and types of goods collected as imperial taxes, and also as statistics on peoples of the empire, their populations, movements and tax quotas.

Below: The Incas and Spaniards were curious about each other. Asked what the Spaniard eats, the reply is 'gold' (Poma de Ayala, Nueva Corónica, c.1615).

Much information in early Spanish sources comes from consultations with *quipucamayoqs*. For example, in the 1560s and 1570s Sarmiento de Gamboa interviewed more than 100 *quipucamayoqs* to compile an Inca history for the viceroy of Peru; and in 1608 Melchior Carlos Inca, a claimant of the Inca throne, compiled the *Relación de los Quipucamayoqs* using the testimonies of four elderly *quipucamayoqs* recorded in 1542.

A second group of record-keepers, called *amautas*, were court historians who memorized the deeds of the emperors, ancient legends and religious information, which they passed down through generations of *amautas*. They, too, provided information for Spanish sources.

Finally, Inca priests had a detailed knowledge of the gods and their relationships, and of ceremony and ritual. They knew the sacred sites and pathways (*ceques*), and the movements of the sun, moon, Venus, Pleiades and Milky Way. Local priests knew their sacred sites (*huacas*), of which there were thousands throughout the empire.

SPANISH RECORDS

The only written records, therefore, date from after the Spanish Conquest. They include: Spanish conquistador accounts; records of the Catholic clergy as they converted native Andeans to Christianity; records of Spanish administrative officials as they organized their conquered subjects for labour and taxation; legal documents of colonial court actions; and personal letters and histories written by native and Spanish individuals to describe their own lives and views, or to summarize Inca religion and history. These sources reveal much information about Inca daily life, social and political organization and religious beliefs.

First-hand accounts based on direct observation at the time of writing are known as primary sources. Chief among these is the native Felipe Guaman Poma

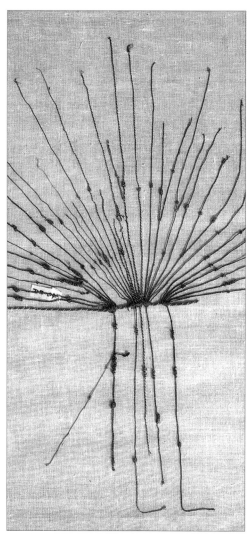

Above: A typical Inca quipu *of tied and dyed knotting, used as a record and memory aid by Inca record-keepers.*

de Ayala's *El Premier Nueva Corónica y Buen Gobierno*, written 1584–1615. He describes Inca life in great detail, protests to the king of Spain about the treatment of the Incas and graphically represents Inca life and religion in 398 drawings.

By contrast, works written by authors using the information in primary sources are known as secondary sources. A principal secondary source is Father Bernabé Cobo's *Historia del Nuevo Mundo* (1653), which includes *Inca Religion and Customs*. Cobo used the works of, among others, Juan Polo de Ondegardo (1560s and 70s), from which he completed the list of Cuzco shrines and *ceques*, and Garcilasco de la Vega ('El Inca'), son of a conquistador and Inca princess, who wrote a commentary on the Inca imperial household and a general history of the Spanish Conquest. Cobo's monumental 20-year work is considered the most balanced and comprehensive early account of Inca history and religion.

APPROACH WITH CAUTION

Such records must be used with caution, however. Each writer, native or Spaniard, was writing from his own cultural point of view and did not fully understand the institutions and social structure of the other. Each inevitably interpreted information about the other from his own viewpoint.

For example, however comprehensive Poma de Ayala's nearly 1,200-page compilation is, his family, originally from

Above: A 16th-century Spanish caravel sailing for the New World. The caravel was a fast and easily manoeuvrable ship with a gently sloping bow and a single stern castle.

Below: After Pizarro's treachery and capture of Atahualpa at Cajamarca there followed many fierce battles between Inca armies and the Spaniards, here against Francisco Hernández Girón (Poma de Ayala, c.1615).

Huanuco in the Central Highlands, had been forcibly relocated by the Incas to Huamango (Ayacucho). In addition, members of his family served as *quipucamayoqs* and he himself converted to Christianity and became an interpreter for Spanish administrative and ecclesiastical inspectors. He therefore bore a grudge against the Incas, abhorred the persistence of Andean religious practices, and at the same time protested about the brutality of Spanish treatment of his fellow natives (frequently shown in his depictions).

Incas and Spaniards both had ulterior motives for their conquests and considered themselves a superior race. As a result, they sometimes deliberately falsified their accounts to justify their actions. In particular, the main source for Spanish chroniclers was the Incas themselves, more specifically the Inca ruling class. So information about ordinary Incas and their contemporaries (both elite and common citizens), and about pre-Inca cultures were doubly filtered: first through the

Inca elite's preconceptions (in the primary source) and later through Spanish opinions (in the secondary source).

Another note of caution that must be added is the vagueness that pervades places and names in Inca and Spanish writings. Provinces, towns and peoples listed by one traveller differ from those listed by another travelling the same route. There were also widespread movements of peoples over the centuries and by the Incas themselves.

Despite these drawbacks, scholars generally think that the basic events in Inca history were more accurately recorded the closer they occurred to the Spanish Conquest. Also that, by comparing and contrasting several sources describing the same events or information about Inca society, truthful information can be extracted.

EXPLORERS AND THE FIRST ARCHAEOLOGISTS

Early Spanish writings primarily concern the Incas, which leaves our principal source of information about pre-Inca Andean civilization to be archaeology. Until the material remains of ancient sites were explored and excavated there was much speculation but little substance to writings about ancient Andean cultures.

ARCHAEOLOGICAL EXPLORERS

Alexander von Humboldt was the first scholar seriously to consider reasons for the presence of humans in the New World and to attempt to make a record of the ancient ruins he saw in the Andes. He was a pioneer, struggling to separate observation and description from speculation and interpretation.

The first dedicated report on ancient Andean antiquities was that of Mariano Edward de Rivero and John James von Tschudi in 1841. Inspired by antiquarian activities and publications in Europe and North America, Rivero had been appointed director of Peru's national museum in Lima, where antiquities from all over Peru were collected. The two made a systematic record of what was known.

William Prescott's *History of the Conquest of Peru* (1847) did much to inspire enthusiasm for ancient Andean civilization, but by and large did not consider archaeological material. Johann Tschudi's five-volume *Reisen durch Süd Amerika* (1869) and Ephraim G. Squier's *Peru: Incidents of Travel and Exploration in the Land of the Incas* (1877) echo the travels of John Stephens and Frederick Catherwood in Mesoamerica.

These and other early attempts to write about ancient Andean civilization lacked a methodological approach to relate the archaeological materials and ruins to contexts. It was soon realized that the ruins themselves must be explored beyond mere descriptions of their surface remains, and that study of ancient Andean artefacts must go further than collection from looted tombs and description.

THE FIRST EXCAVATORS

One of the earliest deliberate excavations was undertaken by Alphons Stübel and Wilhelm Reiss. At the ancient cemetery of Ancón, north of Lima, they excavated unlooted tombs containing mummy

Above: An early 20th-century photograph of the 'Sun Gate' at Tiwanaku shows it cracked and collapsing. The entire gateway is actually a single monolithic carved block, now repaired.

bundles, thus gaining primary information on burial practices and their contents in context. They published their finds and interpretations in three volumes in *The Necropolis of Ancón in Peru* between 1880 and 1887.

Similarly, Adolph Bandelier carried out excavations of Tiwanaku sites on the islands in the Titicaca Basin, which he published in 1910, and at Tiwanaku itself in 1911. On the Island of the Sun in Titicaca, at the site of Chucaripupata, he found gold, silver, bronze and copper artefacts, including a golden mask, near the sacred rock of Titikala.

The work of Stübel and Reiss inspired a young fellow German, Max Uhle. After studying philology, Uhle switched to archaeology and ethnography and became curator at the Dresden Museum. He met Stübel and collaborated with him to publish *Die Ruinenstätte von Tiahuanaco* in 1892, based on the records and photographs Stübel had made at Tiwanaku. Uhle began his own fieldwork in Peru in the same year and continued until 1912. He was the first to apply the archaeological principles of stratigraphy (assessing

Left: Air geysers at Turbaco, from the work of Alexander von Humboldt (1769–1859), the German naturalist and explorer.

Above: A fanciful engraving of Cuzco, the Inca capital, by the German cartographer Georg Braun, 1594. Pizarro called it "the most noble and great city" when he entered it on 23 March 1534.

the chronology of finds from their positions in the earth) in his excavations. With his knowledge of Inca and Tiwanaku pottery types, his excavations at Pachacamac on the Peruvian coast enabled him to construct the first pre-Inca chronology of ancient Andean ceramics. Knowing that Inca pottery was dated to the 15th and 16th centuries, and that the Incas revered the monuments of ancient Tiwanaku, he reasoned that Tiwanaku ceramics pre-dated the Incas. The pottery he excavated at Pachacamac was often found in the same layers as Inca pottery, but showed no stylistic influence from Tiwanaku. He reasoned that it must be intermediate in date between the two. This was the beginning of 30 years of excavation and analysis in Peru, Bolivia, Ecuador and Chile, during which he used the relative dating method of seriation to provide a chronology of ancient Andean ceramic styles that basically remains valid today.

A 20TH-CENTURY EXPLORER

Adventurous exploration, however, had not ended. Prescott had inspired many, including Hiram Bingham. Young Bingham had gone to Peru in 1911 on a romantic dream. "Archaeology lies outside my field and I know very little about the Incas, except the fascinating story told by Prescott in his famous *Conquest of Peru*", he declared to the Peruvian Prefect whose *Departamento* he wanted to explore.

Inca imperial Machu Picchu became 'lost' after the Spanish Conquest only because of its remote location. (Colonial records refer to the site and local people knew it well.) Although Bingham always claimed that he wandered by chance up the newly opened road from Cuzco to the north-west towards the Amazon, in fact, Melchor Artega, a local farmer, described the site to Bingham when he and his team arrived in the Urubamba Valley. Artega, Sergeant Carrasco, Bingham's Quechua translator, and a boy even acted as guides. Nevertheless it was Bingham who brought the spectacular find to the attention of the Western world and solved the 'mystery' of the famous site. To his credit, he did not stop there,

Below: A classic view of the Machu Picchu ruins, the Inca imperial retreat and sacred city in the remote Andes north-west of Cuzco.

Above: Alexander von Humboldt, explorer, geographer, naturalist and lecturer, the first person to make a thorough scientific exploration of the Andes, including its archaeological ruins.

but continued to explore, and in his single summer season made several more discoveries of remote Inca sites.

Bingham's 'discovery' of Machu Picchu, for better or worse, will remain one of the most important events in the annals of Andean archaeology, and it made him a celebrity: he became an Ivy League professor, an Air Force hero and was elected to the US Senate.

20TH-CENTURY ARCHAEOLOGY AND BEYOND

The early 20th century was an age of discovery, large-scale excavation and development of scientific archaeology. Grand multi-disciplinary research programmes were undertaken in the Andes, and Alfred Kroeber and John Rowe of the University of California, Berkeley, refined and expanded Max Uhle's chronological scheme, defining the Periods and Horizons of Andean prehistory. The discovery of radiocarbon dating by Willard Libby enabled calendar dates to be fixed at many sites.

GRAND PROJECTS

Universities, museums and research organizations with enormous resources funded large-scale survey projects and excavations through multiple field seasons. Archaeologists began to ask specific questions about Andean civilization and to undertake work designed to answer them. They went beyond exploration and description to analysis and interpretation,

Below: An adobe brick-lined Nazca shaft tomb, used for the repeated deposition of honoured elite – part of the cult of ancestor worship.

not only of the detailed prehistoric Andean events but also of mechanisms and explanations of why domestication occurred, and why cities arose.

Increasing collections of pottery, metalwork, textiles and other materials prompted the development of methods for conserving and restoring them. This work provided increasingly sophisticated information, making possible complex interpretations that went beyond technology to provide explanations about ancient religion, politics and social structure.

Julio Tello, a native Peruvian, studied archaeology and anthropology at Harvard University, followed by a lifelong career, beginning in the 1920s, investigating the origins of Andean civilization through excavations at the Paracas cemeteries, Sechín Alto and Chavín de Huántar. With Kroeber, he established the Institute of Andean Research in Lima in 1939.

The Second World War only briefly interrupted such studies. Scholars in the 1950s and 1960s extended the reach of projects to all periods of Andean prehistory, until the huge amount of discovery and interpretation required collation and

Above: Moche Huaca del Sol, made of millions of adobe mud bricks. In plan it formed a thick-armed cross, largely destroyed by Spaniards looking for buried treasure.

systemization. In 1969 the Peruvian archaeologist Luis Lumbreras produced the first great synthesis of Peruvian prehistory, *The Peoples and Cultures of Ancient Peru* (translated into English by Betty Meggers in 1974); and in 1971 Gordon Willey published the second volume of his monumental *An Introduction to American Archaeology: South America*.

The increasing fieldwork and accelerating pace of analysis and interpretation during the later 20th and 21st centuries required renewed synthesis. Most notable is Michael Moseley's *The Incas and their Ancestors: The Archaeology of Peru*, published in 1992, then revised in 2001.

REVOLUTION?

A 'revolution' dubbed 'New Archaeology' in the 1960s and 70s applied wider theoretical concepts to archaeological data. Scholars increasingly questioned the system of methods and principles that were used in archaeology and posed deeper questions about alleged cultural universals. This healthy internal analysis happily did not deter fieldwork and data accumulation through excavations and field surveys continued. Archaeologists continue to ask wide questions as well as conduct detailed analysis and interpretation

in specific areas and specialized topics, so expanding our overall understanding of Andean prehistory.

LINES OF ENQUIRY

The Nazca lines have fascinated generations. In the 1940s, Paul and Rose Kosok expounded their theory that the lines were astronomically motivated. Maria Reiche, inspired by the Kosoks, became 'queen of the pampa' and devoted her life to the astronomical cause. Her particular contribution was the extensive mapping of lines, especially the figures. Neither the Kosoks nor Reiche, however, could prove their astronomical theories with convincing statistical evidence.

In the 1970s and 80s, the archaeo-astronomer Frank Aveni conducted the most extensive survey and study of Nazca geoglyphs yet made. He found no statistically significant correlations or directional correlations. Instead, he found 62 nodes from which lines radiated, and discovered there are many generations of lines, earlier ones crossing older ones, concluding that they were for ritual processions, made over generations for specific occasions.

SHAKEN REVELATIONS

In 1950, an earthquake flattened much of Cuzco, including the Dominican church and monastery. Reconstruction of the monastery provided an opportunity to investigate the Coricancha temple beneath, so priority was given to exposing the Inca remains.

Above: Archaeologists of the Instituto Nacional de Cultura uncover the skeleton of one of 72 Inca battle victims in a mass burial at Puruchuco, a suburb of Lima.

Excavations in the monastery plaza revealed an Inca cobblestone floor and wall foundations on the southern and northern sides. With John Rowe's map based on colonial documents, excavators Oscar Ladrón de Guevera and Raymundo Béjar Navarro, together with architectural historians Graziano Gasparini and Luise Margolies, were able to plan and illustrate the appearance of the sacred temple. Much of the monastery ruins were removed and the Coricancha complex was reconstructed, as seen today.

CONTINUED DISCOVERIES

Despite the wealth of Andean metalwork, ceramics and textiles in museums, there is no greater treasure than a collection of such artefacts found *in situ*. The discovery of unlooted Moche tombs at Sipán in the Lambayeque Valley in the late 1980s by Walter Alva and Susana Meneses was just that. Having heard about a *huaquero* raid on the Sipán pyramid, the police in turn raided the robbers' house and recovered artefacts the robbers had taken. The

Left: Ruins of part of the Kalasasaya sacred temple compound at Tiwanaku, Bolivia. They have since been re-erected and the compound partly reconstructed.

police chief then phoned Alva, and under armed guard he and Meneses excavated the low platform at the foot of the pyramid, where they discovered six burial levels, including the fabulously rich tombs of the Lord of Sipán, a Moche priest and the Old Lord of Sipán.

In 2002, the ironically named shanty-town of Tupac Amaru (last 'Inca' emperor, 1571–2) on Lima's outskirts was being cleared for redevelopment. Following modern practice, archaeological investigations preceded, during which an Inca cemetery of up to 10,000 burials was discovered. Some 2,000 burials of men, women and children were recovered, together with 60,000 artefacts, including 40 elite mummy bundles with 'false heads', some with wigs! These finds – everyday items, utensils and food, personal valuables – are being analysed. Their value for the reconstruction of Inca burial practices and everyday life are incalculable.

Even more recently, in 2007, a remarkable discovery was made in the Puruchuco suburb of Lima: a mass grave of 72 bodies killed in battle in 1536. The skull of one drew immediate attention: it was of a young Inca warrior, and it had two round holes in it. Near it was a small plug of bone with musket-ball markings, and electron microscopy detected traces of lead in the skull! It was the first time that evidence of death by gunshot – an Inca shot by a Spaniard – had ever been found in the Americas.

TIMELINE OF THE INCAS AND THEIR ANCESTORS

CHRONOLOGY OF ANDEAN AREA CIVILIZATION

The chronology of the Andean Area is complex. Archaeologists have developed a scheme based on technological achievements and on changing political organization through time, from the first arrival of humans in the area (15,000–3500BC) to the conquest of the Inca Empire by Francisco Pizarro in 1532. The pace of technological development varied in different regions within the Andean Area, especially in early periods in its history. The development of lasting and strong contact between regions, however, spread both technology and ideas and led to regions depending on each other to some degree. Sometimes this interdependence was due to large areas being under the control of one 'authority', while at other times the unifying link was religious or based on trade/technology.

The principal chronological scheme for the Andean Area comprises a sequence of eight time units: five Periods and three Horizons. Periods are defined as times when political unity across regions was less consolidated. Smaller areas were controlled by city-states, sometimes in loose groupings,

perhaps sharing religious beliefs despite having different political views. The Horizons, by contrast, were times when much larger political units were formed. These units exercised political, economic and religious control over extended areas, usually including different types of terrain rather than being confined to coastal valley groups or sierra city-states.

Different scholars give various dates for the beginnings and endings of the Periods and Horizons, and no two books on Andean civilization give exactly the same dates. The durations of Periods and

Above: The walled royal compounds of the Chimú capital Chan Chan.

Horizons also vary from one region to another within the Andean Area, and the charts have increased in complexity as authors have divided the Andean Area into coastal, sierra and Altiplano regions, or even into north, central and southern coastal regions and north, central and southern highland regions. The dates given here are a compilation from several sources, thus avoiding any anomalies in any specific sources.

CHRONOLOGICAL PERIOD	DATES	PRINCIPAL CULTURES
Lithic / Archaic Period	15,000–3500BC	spread of peoples into the Andean Area hunter-gatherer cultures
Preceramic / Formative Period (Cotton Preceramic)	3500–1800BC	early agriculture and first ceremonial centres
Initial Period	1800–750BC	U-shaped ceremonial centres, platform mounds and sunken courts
Early Horizon	750–200BC	Chavín, Paracas, Pukará (Yaya-Mama) cults
Early Intermediate Period	200BC–AD600	Moche, Nazca and Titicaca Basin confederacies
Middle Horizon	AD600–1000	Wari and Tiwanaku empires
Late Intermediate Period	AD1000–1400	Chimú and Inca empires
Late Horizon	AD1400–1532	Inca Empire and Spanish Conquest

LITHIC / ARCHAIC PERIOD (15,000–3500BC)

Above: View from the Cuz del Condor showing the mountains and valleys of Peru.

Ice-free corridors open up across the Bering Strait *c*.40,000 to *c*.20,000 years ago, but there is no evidence that humans entered the New World until the late stages of this time period.

c.20,000BC Migrating hunter-gatherers, using stone-, bone-, wood- and shell-tool technologies, probably entered the New World from north-east Asia.

from *c*.15,000 years ago Palaeoindians migrated south and east to populate North and South America, reaching Monte Verde in southern Chile *c*.14,850 years ago.

c.8500–5000BC Andean and Altiplano hunter-gatherers occupy cave and rock shelter sites in the Andes (e.g. Pachamachay, Guitarrero, Tres Ventanas and Toquepala caves). Evidence of tending of hemp-like fibre, medicinal plants, herbs and wild tubers.

c.6000BC–*c*.5500BC The first true monumental structures, two long parallel mounds, are built at Nanchoc, a late Archaic Period valley in the Zana Valley, north-west Peru.

by 5000BC plant domestication, as opposed to tending wild plants, is truly underway in the highlands.

c.5000BC The Chinchorros peoples make the first deliberately mummified burials in the Atacama Desert.

PRECERAMIC / FORMATIVE PERIOD (3500–1800BC)

Above: Alpaca grazing in the Valle de Coloa. Camelids were herded c.3500–1800BC.

This period is sometimes also called the Cotton Preceramic.

c.3500–1800BC True plant domestication of cotton, squashes, gourds, beans, maize, potatoes, sweet potatoes and chillies. Llamas and other camelids herded on the Altiplano.

c.3500BC Valdivians found Real Alto.

c.3200BC First ceramics made by Valdivian farmers in coastal Ecuador.

by 3000BC the full range of major food plants is grown in the highlands and the guinea pig is bred for meat.

c.3000BC Coastal villages such as Huaca Prieta flourish, producing early textiles.

c.2700BC Early northern coastal civic-ceremonial centres at Aspero – Huaca de los Idolos and Huaca de los Sacrificios.

by 2500BC the llama and alpaca have been truly domesticated.

c.2500BC Clay figurines at Huaca de los Idolos, Aspero.

c.2500–2000BC Large raised mound platforms constructed at El Paraíso, La Galagada and Kotosh.

c.2000BC Carved gourds at Huaca Prieta. Earliest coastal and highland pottery. Loom and heddle weaving begins.

INITIAL PERIOD (1800–750BC)

Above: The U-shaped ceremonial centre of Chavín de Huántar began c.900BC.

Spread of pottery, irrigation agriculture, monumental architecture, religious processions and ritual decapitation.

from *c*.1800BC Sophisticated irrigation systems developed in coastal oases, valleys, the highlands and Altiplano.

c.1800BC Construction at Moxeke includes colossal adobe heads.

c.1750BC Builders at La Florida bring the first pottery to this region.

c.1500BC Cerro Sechín flourishes as a major highland town.

c.1500BC Earliest Andean gold foil made at Waywaka, Peruvian highlands.

c.1459–1150BC Hammered gold and copper foil at Mina Perdida, coastal Peru.

c.1400–1200BC Sechín Alto becomes the largest U-shaped civic-ceremonial centre in the New World.

c.1300BC The five platform mounds at Cardál are erected.

c.1200BC Carved lines of warriors at Cerro Sechín show regional conflict.

c.1000BC The El Paraíso Tradition flourishes in the Rimac Valley.

c.900BC Earliest U-shaped ceremonial complex at Chavín de Huántar begins.

EARLY HORIZON (750–200BC)

Above: The Paracas Peninsula, which was a necropolis site for several settlements.

Religious cults develop around Chavín de Huántar and Pukará. Decapitation, hallucinogenic drug use and ancestor worship become widespread.

*c.*800BC Sechín Alto abandoned as a ceremonial centre.

from *c.*750BC The Old Temple at Chavín established as a cult centre. Influence of the Lanzón deity and the Staff Deity spreads. The Paracas Peninsula serves as a necropolis site, and the Oculate Being is depicted on textiles and ceramics.

*c.*500BC Construction of the New Temple at Chavín de Huántar begins.

*c.*500BC Earliest known fired-clay discs for pottery vessel making, Paracas.

*c.*400–200BC The Old Temple at Chavín enlarged to create the New Temple. The Chavín Cult spreads, especially at Kuntur Wasi and Karwa (Paracas).

*c.*400BC Annual rainfall levels fall in the Titicaca Basin. Pukará becomes centre of the Yaya-Mama Cult.

*c.*350 to 200BC Highland regional conflict evident in fortress-building in the Santa, Casma and Nepeña valleys.

*c.*250BC Beginning of the first settlement at Tiwanaku in the Titicaca Basin.

*c.*200BC Influence of Chavín Cult wanes.

EARLY INTERMEDIATE PERIOD (200BC–AD600)

Above: Construction of the Moche Huaca del Sol began c.AD100.

Cohesion of the Chavín Cult disintegrates, and several regional chiefdoms develop in the coastal and mountain valleys.

*c.*100BC Rise of the Nazca in the southern Peruvian coastal valleys and Cahuachi founded.

*c.*AD100 Burial of the Old Lord of Sipán in Lambayeque Valley.

*c.*AD100 Sacred ceremonial centre of Cahuachi dominates the Nazca area.

*c.*1st century AD Moche dynasty founded in the northern coastal valleys.

*c.*AD100 Construction of first temple platforms at Huaca del Sol and Huaca de la Luna at Moche begins.

*c.*AD250 Construction of first temple at Pachacamac and start of the Pachacamac Cult. Major construction of temple platforms at Tiwanaku begins.

*c.*AD300 Burial of the Lord of Sipán in Lambayeque Valley.

AD300–550 Several Moche regional cities founded at Huancaco, Pamapa de los Incas, Pañamarca and Mocollope.

*c.*AD500 The Moche ceremonial platforms of the Huacas del Sol and de la Luna were the largest in the area.

*c.*AD700 Moche/Nazca power wanes.

MIDDLE HORIZON (AD600–1000)

Above: View of wall and monolithic stelae, Semi-Subterranean Court, Tiwanaku.

Much of the Andean Area unified in two empires: Tiwanaku in the south and Wari in the north.

*c.*AD200 Major phase of monumental construction begins at Tiwanaku.

*c.*AD250 Settlement at Huari founded.

*c.*AD300 Major construction of central ceremonial plaza at Tiwanaku begins.

*c.*AD400–750 Elite residential quarters at Tiwanaku built. Tiwanaku colonies established at San Pedro Atacama, Omo and in the Cochabamba Valley.

*c.*AD500 Major construction at Huari and beginning of domination of the central highlands by the Wari Empire.

*c.*AD550 Pampa Grande flourishes, ruled by Sicán Lords.

by *c.*AD600 the cities of Huari and Tiwanaku dominate the highlands, building empires in the central and highlands Altiplano, respectively.

*c.*AD650 Wari city of Pikillacta founded, and Wari colonies established at Jincamocco, Azángaro, Viracochapampa and Marca Huamachuco.

*c.*AD750–1000 Third major phase of palace building begins at Tiwanaku.

*c.*AD850–900 Pikillacta abandoned.

LATE INTERMEDIATE PERIOD (AD1000–1400)

Above: View of present-day Cuzco and the Cuzco Valley where the Incas settled.

An era of political break-up is characterized by the rise of new city-states, including Lambayeque, Chimú and Pachacamac, the Colla and Lupaka kingdoms, and numerous city-states in the central and southern Andean valleys.

*c.*AD900–950 Rise of the Lambayeque-Sicán state in northern coastal Peru. Burial of the Sicán Lords at Lambayeque. Sicán capital city at Batán Grande.

*c.*AD950 Sediments of Lake Titicaca show evidence of decreased rainfall and start of a long period of drought leading to the eventual demise of Tiwanaku.

*c.*AD900 Chan Chan, capital of the Chimú, founded in the Moche Valley.

*c.*AD1000 Tiwanaku and Wari empires wane as regional political rivalry reasserts itself.

*c.*AD1000 Huari city-state abandoned.

*c.*1100 The Incas under Manco Capac, migrate into the Cuzco Valley, found Cuzco and establish the Inca dynasty.

*c.*1250 City of Tiwanaku abandoned, perhaps because of changes in climate.

*c.*1300 Sinchi Roca becomes the first emperor to use the title Sapa Inca.

*c.*1350 The Chimú conquer the Lambayeque-Sicán peoples.

LATE HORIZON (AD1400–1532)

Above: Inca stonework is distinctive in style and among the finest in the world.

In little more than 130 years the Incas build a huge empire, from Colombia to mid-Chile and from the rainforest to the Pacific and establish an imperial cult centred on Inti, the sun god, whose representative on Earth was the Sapa Inca.

*c.*1425 Viracocha, the eighth ruler, begins the Inca conquests and domination of the Cuzco Valley.

1438 Pachacuti Inca Yupanqui defeats the Chancas to dominate the Cuzco Valley and begin the expansion of the Inca Empire both within and outside the valley.

1438–71 Pachacuti begins his rebuilding of Cuzco as the imperial capital to the plan of a crouching puma, with the fortress and sun temple of Sacsahuaman forming the puma's head.

*c.*1450 Pachacuti establishes the city of Machu Picchu.

c.1462 Pachacuti begins the conquest of the Kingdom of Chimú.

1471 The Incas conquer the Kingdom of Chimú.

1471–93 Inca Tupac Yupanqui expands the empire west and south, doubling its size – north as far as the present-day Ecuador–Colombia border and south into the Titicaca Basin.

Above: The city of Machu Picchu, founded by Pachacuti c.1450.

1493–1526 Huayna Capac consolidates the empire, building fortresses, road systems, storage redistribution and religious precincts throughout the provinces. The provincial city of Qenqo is founded.

1526 Huayna Capac dies of smallpox without an agreed successor.

1526–32 Huayna Capac's son Huáscar seizes the throne but is challenged by his brother Atahualpa. A six-year civil war ends in the capture of Huáscar.

1530 Inca Empire at its greatest extent, and the largest territory in the world.

1532 Francisco Pizarro lands with a small Spanish army on the north coast of the Inca Empire and marches to meet Atahualpa at Cajamarca. He exploits the disruption of the civil war to play one claimant against the other.

1532 The Spaniards defeat the Incas at the Battle of Cajamarca and capture Atahualpa, holding him for ransom.

1533 Atahualpa condemned in a rigged Spanish trial and executed for adultery and idolatry.

1535 Francisco Pizarro founds Lima as his capital in Spanish Peru.

1541 Pizarro assassinated in his palace at Lima by Almagro and his associates.

CHAPTER ONE

LIVING IN THE LANDSCAPE

The diverse landscapes of South America were created by geological processes, and the varied fauna and flora developed as a result of biological evolution. South America includes multiple environmental and ecological zones. Its fauna and flora evolved independently from about 175 million years ago in the middle Jurassic Period, after the super-continent of Pangaea (Antarctica, Australia, India, Africa, Eurasia, and North and South America) began to divide into today's continents. Through remote periods of physical isolation from North America, the flora and fauna of the continent evolved into unique groups and species, which were later mutually exchanged with North America when the landmasses were ultimately reconnected. This combination of events created the landscapes and plant and animal life encountered by the first human migrants into South America as the great Ice Ages of the northern hemisphere ended.

Social evolution created the ultimate sophistication of Andean civilization, which enabled the Incas to create an empire that controlled the largest territory in the world at the time of the Spanish arrival in the New World.

This chapter describes both these worlds – the physical and the socio-political – as they were when an intrepid and determined group of men from the Old World reached the New World of the South American continent in a second episode of migration. This time, it was a clash of urban empires.

Left: The upper Urubamba–Vilcanote River, Peru, a sacred mountain valley whose rich soils are especially productive.

LANDSCAPES OF THE ANDEAN AREA

South America has evolved animal and plant species unique to its regions owing to long periods of physical isolation from North America. Towards the end of the Pliocene Epoch, *c.*3 million years ago, the Central American ridge re-emerged above sea level to reunite North and South America, creating a land bridge for their long-separated mammals.

GEOGRAPHICAL REGIONS

South America includes several major ecological and environmental regions that merge into each other across the breadth and length of the continent: the great western coastal deserts, pierced by scores of oases valleys and their rivers flowing into the Pacific Ocean; the Andean mountain range, winding the entire length of the continent, 7,500km (4,660 miles) from the Caribbean to Tierra del Fuego; the more gradual descent of the eastern Andes; the high Altiplano between the two Andean cordilleras and pampas to the south and east; and the huge Amazon Basin. There are also the rich maritime seascapes of the Pacific, Atlantic and Caribbean coastal waters.

Prehistorians subdivide the continent into zones of cultural development, each characterized by distinct archaeological

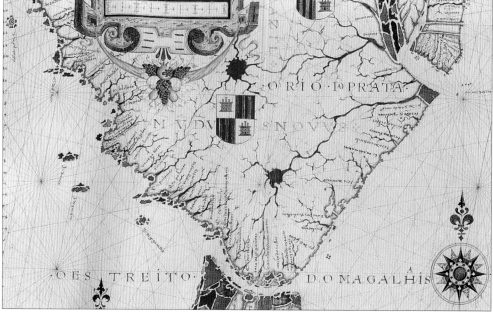

Above: South America and the Magellan Straits from the Hydrographic Atlas *of 1571 by Fernan Vaz Dourado.*

evidence and levels of technological and socio-political achievement. None of these zones was culturally isolated, and inter-relationships between zones were never static, but changed through time. The zone with which this book is concerned is the Andean Area. It comprises, west to east, the Pacific coast to the Amazonian Rainforest, and, north to south, roughly the modern Colombian–Ecuadorian border to the northern half of Chile.

THE ANDEAN AREA

The Andean Area is remarkable for its contrasting landscapes, both geographical and cultural. It includes the world's driest deserts, such as the Sechura in northern Peru–Ecuador, the Nazca in central Peru and the Atacama in northern Chile; some of the world's highest mountains, with peaks of more than 7,000m (23,000ft); and some of the lushest rainforests along the eastern edge of the Amazon Basin.

Climatic conditions vary greatly within the zone. El Niño events disrupt weather patterns and marine cycles about every four to ten years, reversing normal patterns by creating floods in coastal regions and drought in the mountains and Altiplano. Throughout Andean history there were

intermittent periods of prolonged drought, coinciding with the cultural periods defined by archaeologists. Evidence from glacial ice cores and lake sediments show sustained drought periods occurring *c.*2200–1900BC, 900–800BC, 400–200BC, AD1–300, AD562–95 and

Below: An Andean mountain peak, Mount Huayna Potosi, Bolivia, with abundant snow most of the year, from which flow waters to make mountain valleys fertile.

Below: The Atacama Desert, northern Chile, is one of the driest places on Earth – high and dry, with sparse, tough vegetation.

Above: Lush Amazonian rainforests flank the eastern Andes. The Incas considered their inhabitants to be subhuman.

AD1100–1450; and intervening wetter periods c.AD400–500, AD900–1000 and 1500–1700.

There was also great cultural variation. People developed distinct responses to different landscapes and environments, and distinct cultures. They evolved from wandering hunter-gatherers to early village farming communities as they selected and nurtured certain plants and animals into domestication. Finally, as they developed and mastered increasingly sophisticated socio-political and techno-logical techniques, they evolved into civilizations with spreading towns and cities, kingdoms and even empires.

CIVILIZATION

Archaeologists are involved in never-ending examination and discussion of what defines civilization and what stimulates its devel-opment. Civilization of the highest calibre was attained in the Andean Area, and it evolved in part in response to the chal-lenges presented by its varied landscapes.

Its Pacific coasts are the world's rich-est fishing grounds, the consequence of the cold Humboldt Current that sweeps up from Antarctica and brings huge fish shoals and migrating sea mammals, as well as nurturing rich coastal shellfish and bird populations. There is such abundance that the earliest inhabitants could support large village populations mostly reliant

Right: A high Andean lake valley, the Laguna Colorado, Bolivia, provided abundant flamingos to be hunted.

on the foreshore and near offshore waters for their livings. The river valleys descend-ing from the western Andean foothills to the coastal plains have rich soils on which early peoples learned to practise increas-ingly intense and sophisticated irrigation agriculture. Similarly, in high Andean val-leys and the Altiplano, people graduated from simple rainfall agriculture to increas-ingly intense cultivation using raised fields, hillside terracing and irrigation systems. On the rich grasslands of the southern Andean plateaux, people devel-oped pastoralism with the domestication of the llama and alpaca.

INTERREGIONAL RELATIONS

These developments in agriculture, which led to trading between different regions, and the technological and socio-political advances they stimulated, enabled pop-ulations to increase, so that larger towns and cities came into being. Remarkable throughout Andean prehistory is the con-tinuity of contact between the different regions, beginning from the earliest times, as proved by the discovery of products and raw materials from different regions in the others.

There was exchange between the high-lands and lowlands in both physical objects and ideas. For example, coastal

Above: Vast high grasslands of the southern Andean Altiplano provided an ideal environment for llama and alpaca herding.

products, such as oyster shells, were regarded as exotic treasures among moun-tain cultures. Reciprocally, early coastal textiles were made of the cotton grown locally, and of llama wool traded from Altiplano herders. People also borrowed and exchanged artistic expressions and symbolism between regions. This is demonstrated by the spread of the Chavín Staff Deity from the central highlands to southern desert coasts and the Altiplano; by the recognition by coastal peoples of the sacredness of the mountains, no doubt fostered by a realization that mountains were the ultimate source of their water, and their construction of man-made 'mountains' in the form of huge pyrami-dal platforms; and by the representation of rainforest animals such as monkeys and caymans in Nazca lines and in Chavín stone sculpture.

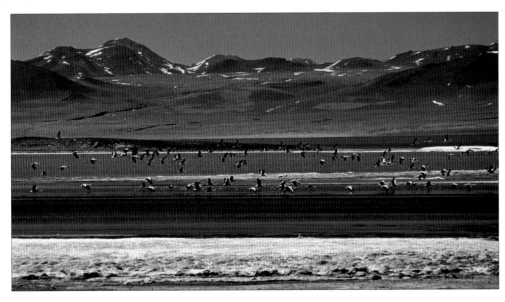

PLANTS IN THE ANDEAN AREA

Tens of thousands of plant species evolved in South America: grasses and reeds; tropical and western forest trees; cacti; fungi; herbal plants and flowers; and a variety of wild edible fruits and vegetables. Different environments within the Andean Area provided a rich diversity and potential cultigens. Microclimates created by altitude change and latitude provided pockets and refuges for different species.

VEGETATION REGIONS

The Pacific coastal environment is one of the world's richest. Oxygen- and nutrient-rich cold currents support the trillions of phytoplankton that form the base of the coastal food chain. Small fishes feed on these microscopic plants, and are fed upon by predatory fishes, and so on up the food chain. Inland, the coastal plain from Ecuador to northern Chile includes vast expanses of almost barren desert.

The Andes include four vegetation zones: tropical, subtropical, south temperate

and *paramo* (between high *puna* grassland and the snowline). Vegetation in the coastal valleys that punctuate the coastal plain changes up-valley as altitude increases.

The western Andean slopes are characterized by temperate forests, found from near sea level to the tree-line. The lower altitudes have broadleaf evergreen trees, while higher up conifers dominate. Species include the algarrobo, lengas, podocarps, the monkey puzzle and cypresses. Dry forests of the southern Bolivian and northern Argentinian Altiplano feature trees of the pea family, together with vast grasslands, known as *puna*, and a large number of cacti species.

As the eastern Andes, known as selva or *montaña*, descend to the Amazon Basin, they are forested by evergreen trees from *c*.3,000m (10,000ft) and lower, to merge with the tropical rainforest. A host of herbal and medicinal plants include the coca (*Erythroxylon coca*), which became so important in Andean religion and in general use to combat high-altitude fatigue and increase stamina.

CULTIVATED PLANTS

Of the vast number of native species, less than 1 per cent was domesticated by ancient Andeans. Discussions of Andean plants important to civilization ultimately focus on this small percentage of cultigens.

The 23 principal pre-Hispanic cultivated species became domesticated through selective tending. Early agriculture relied on run-off water (especially in coastal valleys) and rainfall (especially in the Andes), until irrigation, terracing and raised-field agriculture were developed as means of increasing yields and areas under cultivation.

Left: The interdependence of highland and lowland, east and west, are exemplified in this Chancay carved wooden club – a rainforest monkey holding a maize cob, an essential early domesticated food plant.

Above: Tambopata Reserve, Peru – misty, forested regions of the eastern Andes, known as selva or montaña *– provided valuable herbs and medicinal plants.*

Altitudinal growing ranges of the domestic plants vary, and their distribution across environmental zones stimulated exchange. It is argued that the wild ranges of most cultigens were extended as humans nurtured those species that seemed most promising and able to provide sustainable yields.

Altitude and latitude (and thus temperature and rainfall) affect both cultivation and distribution. Andean

Below: Quinoa (Chanopodium quinoa) was, alongside the potato and maize, one of the earliest and essential domesticated Andean food plants.

domesticated plants can be grouped by their altitudinal ranges – see the fact box below. An extreme example is the ulluco (an edible tuber), which grows at 3,700–3,830m (12,180–12,560ft).

Less than 20 per cent of these crops grow well at altitudes above 3,000m (10,000ft), while 90 per cent thrive up to 1,000m (3,300ft). It is significant that the mainstays of the ancient Andean diet – maize, potatoes and common beans – can be cultivated at the widest possible range of altitudes. The many cultigens of lower altitude, which formed a complementary role to the classic trio in daily lowland and highland diet, were thus an important part of lowland–highland exchange. The staple diet was supplemented by gathering wild and semi-domesticated fruits and nuts, including cashews, pumpkins, palmettos, pineapples, sour cherries, custard apples, cactus fruits, elderberries and an ancient variety of banana. Wild herbs were gathered for seasoning.

DRUGS, TOOLS AND BUILDINGS

In addition to edible plants, medicinal and hallucinogenic plants played an important role in curing illness and for shamanistic trance inducement. Coca was cultivated, but the hallucinogenic mescaline of the San Pedro cactus and many hallucinogenic mushrooms from the tropical forests were also gathered and traded widely. Maize was used for the fermentation of *chicha* beer, the common drink in weak form and used in stronger form in religious ceremony.

Andean trees provided wood for weapons and tools, such as arrow and spear shafts, the *atl-atl* (spear-thrower) and hardwood war clubs. Tools included the foot-plough, sod-breaking club and hoe handle. Coca snuff pallets and drinking cups (*keros*) were also of wood. Algarrobo tree trunks provided pillars and rafters in early Spanish Colonial buildings, preserving an architectural style depicted in numerous Moche ceramic models.

Cane and totora reeds from riverbanks and the shores of Lake Titicaca and other lakes were extensively used for thatching and for fishing craft. Reeds were also used to make flutes and panpipes.

Most textiles for clothing and llama packs were made of cotton and wool. Cotton was indispensable among coastal peoples for fishing gear (nets, line and bindings), while wild fibrous plants

Above: Cacti in Salar de Uyruni Isla Pescado, Bolivia, one of many micro-habitats in the southern Andean Altiplano.

provided the rough twine and cordage needed for rope, baskets and containers, sandals and sleeping mats. The cultivated gourd, which preceded pottery for containers, continued to be used throughout pre-Hispanic times for fishing floats as well.

ANDEAN DOMESTICATED PLANTS BY ALTITUDINAL RANGES

Up to 1,000m (3,300ft)
- arracachas (a tuberous root plant) (850–956m/2,790–3,140ft)
- bottle gourds (850–956m/2,790–3,140ft)
- two varieties of chilli peppers (2–1,000m/6.56–3,300ft and 385–1,000m/1,263–3,300ft)
- guavas (28–1,000m/92–3,300ft)
- lima beans (28–1,000m/92–3,300ft)
- peanuts (46–1,000m/151–3,300ft)
- three varieties of squash (850–969m/2,790–3,179ft, 385–1,000m/1,263–3,300ft and 28–1,000m/92–3,300ft)
- sweet potatoes (28–1,000m/92–3,300ft)
- tobacco (57–1,000m/187–3,300ft)

Just over 1,000m (3,300ft)
- cotton (329–1,006m/1,079–3,300ft)
- manioc (46–1,006m/150–3,300ft)

Middle range
- avocados (320–1,750m/1,049–5,741ft)
- coca (450–1,200m/1,476–3,937ft)
- oca (850–1,700m/2,790–5,577ft)

Very wide range
- beans (2–3,700m/6½–12,140ft)
- maize (2–3,350m/6½–10,990ft)
- potatoes (2–3,830m/6½–12,565ft)
- quinoa (28–3,878m/92–12,720ft)
- mashwa (an edible tuber) (850–3,700m/2,788–12,140ft)
- ulluco (an edible tuber) (3,700–3,830m/12,180–12,560ft)

ANIMALS IN THE ANDEAN AREA

The differing environments within the Andean Area supported a large variety of animal species. As with plants, micro-environments fostered the development of species native to different regions. Remarkable traits of Andean Area fauna are their adaptations to the rarefied air of the mountains and their survival in barren desert environments. Ancient Andean peoples also knew of and revered animals from outside the Andean Area.

FOOD SUPPLIES

The earliest Andean hunter-gatherers would still have had mastodons (the larger mammoths had never reached South America), wild horse and ground sloths to hunt. When these became extinct c.8,000BC, large game animals such as deer (white-tailed, brocket and heumul), the llama and other camelids (vicuña and guanaco) were supplemented

Below: The camelid llama, originally a migrant from the north into temperate South America, once domesticated, provided wool and meat. It was a beast of burden and a sacred symbol to ancient Andeans.

by smaller game such as guinea pigs, viscachas (large burrowing rodents), skunk and fowl.

In contrast, coastal peoples hunted sea mammals (sea lions, seals and whales), supplemented by large and small fish, sea birds and a host of foreshore invertebrates, from molluscs to lobsters and crabs to clams and other shellfish. The principal sources of animal protein after the Lithic and Preceramic periods was provided by coastal fishing and sea mammal hunting, and by fishing in Lake Titicaca and similar high lakes. Fish are scarce in Andean highland rivers.

FOOD CHAINS

The marine animal food chain starts with the smaller fish – especially anchovies and sardines – that feed on phytoplankton, and moves up through ocean birds to sea mammals and, ultimately, humans. There are also shallow-water and foreshore invertebrate herbivores and their attendant predators, from mussels and shellfish to crabs, shorebirds, sea mammals and man.

Inland and in the mountains the ultimate predator is the mountain lion or puma, and in the rainforest and lowlands the jaguar; other top predators are raptors. The chain descends down through increasingly smaller animals to the invertebrates that feed on soil and other detritus.

MIGRATION

There are about 600 mammalian species in South America, dominated by rodents and bats, most of which live in the rainforests. Likewise with birds: the overwhelming variety are tropical; a second group are the western sea and coastal birds; and a third the temperate forest avians and the Andean species, including condors, hawks and the harpy eagle.

The emergence of the Central American land bridge at the end of Pliocene epoch enabled the migration of mammals in both directions between South and North America.

Above: Native burdens were exemplified in Poma de Ayala's Nueva Corónica, c.1615 by symbolic characterization. The royal administrator is a serpent, the itinerant Spaniard a jaguar, the encomendero labour and land-holder a (non-native) lion, the parish priest a fox, the notary a cat, and the native governor a rodent.

Into temperate South America came smilodons (sabretooth cats), wild horses, spectacled bears, tapirs, llamas, peccaries, foxes, rats and mice. Into the tropics came heteromyid rodents, squirrels and shrews.

From south to north temperate environments went giant ground sloths, armadillos, glyptodons (armadillo-like but larger), porcupines and didelphis rodents; and to tropical areas went cebid monkeys, tree sloths, anteaters, and agouti and paca rodents.

North–south migrants added to these existing native mammals, including a wealth of rodents (including the guinea pig), monkeys, bats and the jaguar, as well as a huge number of bird species, reptiles, amphibians and invertebrates. The greatest varieties of all groups are native to the Amazonian Basin, outside the Andean Area.

Right: The revered jaguar (and its mountain cousin the puma) provided a symbol of strength and cunning to Andean warriors and priests.

DOMESTICATED ANIMALS

As with plants, only a few animals were domesticated: llamas, alpacas, guinea pigs, ducks and dogs. The domestication process was gradual, beginning with the deliberate selection and concentrated tending of these species. The main highland sources of meat were guinea pigs and ducks, although llama and deer were also eaten. Hunting, however, had become the pursuit of the elite in a culture whose staple diet was provided by cultivated plant foods.

The llama is one of three South American camelids: llamas, guanacos and vicuñas. The llama is the domesticated variety of the guanaco, which remained wild and was sometimes hunted for its meat, as was the vicuña. A fourth camelid, the alpaca, was also domesticated or semi-domesticated, but it is uncertain if the breed is the result of descent from the guanaco, or a guanaco/vicuña hybrid. Llamas and alpacas, fully domesticated by c.2500BC, were herded in great flocks, principally for their wool and as pack animals, but also for ritual sacrifice, divination and meat. Their bones were valuable for tool-making and their dung for fertilizer.

Below: An 18th-century watercolour of the guinea pig, an early Andean domesticated rodent, which provided a readily available meat source and still does today.

Guinea pigs were domesticated as early as the late Preceramic Period, but this is evident less from anatomical differences to wild relatives than from what appear to be hutches. Hunting of wild guinea pigs for meat no doubt continued. In later pre-Hispanic times the guinea pig was also used in religious ceremony, divination and curing. Ducks were raised for food and eggs; dogs as hunting companions and food.

REVERED ANIMALS

As well as llamas and guinea pigs, several other native Andean and non-native animals were highly revered and used in ritual and prophecy. The flights and habits of condors, hawks and eagles were carefully observed for divination. Indeed, observation of the mobbing and killing of an eagle by buzzards during ceremonies to honour the sun god Inti were regarded by Inca priests as foretelling the coming fall of the empire. The early twined cloth from Preceramic Huaca Prieta features an eagle with outspread wings and a snake inside its stomach.

The puma and its lowland cousin the jaguar also feature in the earliest Andean art. Use of the jaguar in monumental stone sculpture and portable objects in the Chavín Cult right through to the plan of Inca Cuzco in the form of a crouching puma demonstrate its enduring importance.

As well as the jaguar, monkeys, the cayman (South American freshwater alligator), serpents and a great variety of colourful rainforest birds were especially revered for their powers, cleverness and (in the case of the birds) feathers. All feature repeatedly in Andean art in religious contexts and demonstrate long-distance communication between highlands and lowlands.

THE INCA EMPIRE AT PIZARRO'S ARRIVAL

From humble beginnings as one tribe among several in the Cuzco Valley, the Incas rapidly expanded the territory in their control. Their conquests were few in the first few centuries after the founding ruler Manco Capac had established rule in Cuzco. Even by about 1400, Inca territory comprised only the valleys adjacent to the Cuzco Valley in the Urubamba and Apurimac river drainages.

GREAT EXPANSION

From the reign of Pachacuti Inca Yupanqui (tenth emperor, 1438–71) and his successors, however, the Inca emperors embarked on continuous campaigns to subdue the known world. Inca belief taught them that they were destined to rule, and in fewer than 100 years they ruled the largest empire ever created in

Below: Chan Chan, the capital of the Kingdom of the Chimú, was a serious rival to the late 15th-century expanding Inca Empire until it fell to Inca Pachacuti and his son and heir Tupac Yupanqui in 1471.

the Americas. It stretched from the modern borders of Ecuador and Colombia to more than halfway down the coast of modern Chile (4,200km/2,600 miles; equivalent in distance of roughly Spain to Moscow).

Their empire was long and narrow, however (only *c.*650km/400 miles at its greatest east–west width), and confined to regions familiar to them. The Incas were among a long line of cultures that had spread their control of economic resources in the Andes and western coastal lowlands. Their armies were well equipped and disciplined, and were trained to fight on such terrain in pitched battles, during which two armies were amassed and thrown at each other to 'slug it out' until one force broke ranks and fled or laid down their arms in defeat. Indeed, in many cases, as Inca reputation for fighting skills and fierceness, and the seeming inevitability of conquest, spread, many nations (kingdoms and city-states) did not resist, but surrendered without battle and proceeded to negotiate the best deal they could make.

*Above: An Inca post-runner or messenger (*chasqui) *depicted in Poma de Ayala's* Nueva Corónica, c.1615.

AMAZONIAN FAILURE

The Incas attempted to expand east into the Amazon Rainforest. Their armies, however, were in unfamiliar terrain and

faced an enemy who fought unconventionally. In the Amazon, the Incas were not confronting organized states, ruled in a manner similar to the long-developed structures in the Andes. Instead, Amazonian peoples lived in small groups with local chiefs; rather than fight, they simply disappeared into the forest and remained illusive.

The products of the rainforest were obtainable by barter, so there was no reason for the Incas to conquer the land except for the motive of dominating the known world. But they ruled almost all the people whom they considered civilized, and the Amazonians could easily be dismissed as subhuman and therefore incapable of participating in the imperial state structure.

ADMINISTRATIVE GENIUS

A large factor in Inca success was the way in which they treated conquered peoples. Inca provincial governors were placed in charge of the four great divisions of the empire – the four quarters of Tahuantinsuyu – conceived to mimic the four world directions: Antisuyu (north-east), Chinchaysuyu (north-west), Cuntisuyu (south-west) and Collasuyu (south-east). But local rulers and chiefs were normally treated with courtesy and kept in place,

Below: Manco Capac, legendary leader of the Inca people and 'founder' of the empire, depicted in an 18th-century genealogy.

where they were allowed to maintain local control. Their sons were taken as house captives to Cuzco, where they were indoctrinated with Inca values; and their daughters were also taken and indoctrinated – some would be offered as pawns for marriages of alliance with other rulers, though others would be sacrificed.

The genius of the Inca Empire was its administrative organization. Inca civil and economic control was simple in concept and followed developments that had evolved over the past 3,000 years of pre-Hispanic Andean civilization. There was an incremental structure of civic control based on decimal multiples of households, with each higher-ranking official being in charge of ten times more households. Like their concept of the cosmos as a series of layers, this structure presented everyone with a clear line of responsibility from one level to the next.

SOCIAL ORGANIZATION

The Incas intensified and formalized social practices that were ingrained in Andean peoples from early times – the idea of reciprocal obligations and of co-operation with one's kin group of relatives, both blood and by marriage, known as the *ayllu*.

While there was no monetary system, there were taxes and obligations to the state, called the *mit'a*, that amounted to the same thing. Every individual owed labour to the Inca state, which through the *mit'a* was fulfilled by the household rather than by each individual. This left

Above: Huánuca Pampa was typical of Inca regional cities and a great storehouse for the redistribution of imperial tax goods.

the household intact and able to fulfil its obligation at home while some member fulfilled *mit'a* service. Quotas of produce (agricultural or textile) were collected into storehouses for redistribution according to need. In this way the Incas ensured that all their subjects had the necessities of life and so largely forestalled rebellion.

Some rebellions did occur, however, and these were dealt with swiftly. Rebellious groups were moved wholesale to distant provinces, where, in unfamiliar territory and among strangers, they were isolated from their secure social structure. In addition, loyal groups were moved into potentially rebellious areas to keep control. The Inca administrators' skill was in indoctrinating people into a system against which it was futile to resist, and which was in most cases familiar.

All land theoretically belonged to the Inca emperor. It was divided into three parts, the produce of which was given to: the emperor and his household, the Inca state religion and the people themselves. The Incas expanded the land under production, rejuvenating old and constructing new terraces and raised fields. They built provincial storehouse capitals, linked by a road system that made it easy to move goods, and armies, throughout the empire. And they created a messenger service to keep the emperor and his governors informed. This was the empire 'discovered' by Francisco Pizarro.

CIVIL WAR: FALL OF THE INCA EMPIRE

By the early 16th century, the Incas ruled almost all the civilized peoples of South America. The twelfth emperor, Huayna Capac (1493–1526), ruled a stable empire, which he was still expanding. He had gone on campaign to the northern provinces to quell an outbreak of rebellion in the recently subdued Quito province.

STILL EXPANDING

The Incas were aware of the wealth of the gold- and silver-working cultures to the north of the empire. Though not quite the urban civilizations of the Andean Area – many lacked the tradition of stone architecture and conurbation – Colombian metalworking cultures were sophisticated chiefdoms with loose confederations of political power. Whether they would have been easily incorporated into the Inca imperial structure will never be known, however, for in the very year (1526) of Francisco Pizarro's second expedition to the north-west coast of South America,

Below: Hatun Rumiyoc Street, Cuzco, showing the wall of the royal palaces of Inca Roca.

Huayna Capac died of a mysterious disease, as did his chosen heir, Ninancuyuchi. The illness was smallpox, which had been introduced by the Spaniards into Mesoamerica and spread south, ravaging the native populations as it did so because they had no resistance to it.

Huayna Capac's and his heir's deaths were a significant blow to the stability of the empire, which was functioning smoothly despite the very recent acquisition of some territories. Huayna Capac had, in fact, inherited most of the empire he ruled intact and had spent most of his campaign consolidating his inheritance and strengthening the infrastructure. He was particularly engaged in building Inca towns in the northern part of the empire.

DISARRAY AND DISRUPTION

The smooth inheritance that had previously been the case was in disarray. Without a living designated heir, the imperial household was in confusion. Huayna Capac had more than a score of sons, one of whom, Atahualpa, was on campaign with him, while another, Huáscar, he had left in Cuzco as one of four governors. Members of the

Above: The Inca civil war was breaking up the empire when the Spaniards arrived. Camac Inca leads his Inca troops (from Poma de Ayala's Nueva Corónica, *c.1615).*

imperial household quickly divided into factions, each with its own interpretation of what Huayna Capac's intentions had been. They questioned whether Huayna Capac had in fact truly or properly anointed Ninancuyuchi. Huáscar's faction naturally claimed that Huayna Capac intended him to inherit, while Atahualpa's faction claimed that Huayna Capac would have wanted Atahualpa to use his control of the army to take control and maintain the security of the empire in its time of crisis over the succession.

In such unprecedented circumstances, Huáscar seized the throne. At first Atahualpa acknowledged him, but when a local chief spread a rumour that Atahualpa was plotting against Huáscar, the latter declared his half-brother an enemy and traitor and civil war ensued.

The war lasted six years before Atahualpa was finally victorious and had captured and imprisoned Huáscar.

Above: Inca emperor Huayna Capac, 12th Sapa Inca, who died of smallpox, setting off the Inca civil war. From an 18th-century 'Cuzco School' Inca genealogy.

EFFECTS ON THE PEOPLE

The effects of these events on the structure of the empire must have been immense, and the speed of the expansion of the empire would now take its toll. With the imperial armies engaged in fighting each other, recently conquered peoples, especially those far from Cuzco, could cease to acknowledge imperial rule and take back local power.

Soldiers in the army of one or other faction, or people who lived where the fighting between the brothers occurred, would have been directly affected by the war, but most ordinary subjects would have simply carried on making a living. The social structure was, at their level, intact and their households and kinship obligations still operative.

While the events of the civil war were unfolding, there is no evidence of widespread rebellion, just as there was no such outbreak after Atahualpa was executed in 1533. Clearly there was an ingrained inertia in ordinary Andean lives to simply get on with daily routine and lie low. The burdens imposed on them by the Incas – such as the labour tax, textile quotas, the Quechua language and the precedence of the imperial state religion on Inti over local gods – were temporarily relieved, but so too was the structure of the redistribution of goods.

External factors also had an effect, and the spread of smallpox was undoubtedly of more immediate concern. It devastated the peoples in the area that had been the northern Kingdom of Chimú shortly after the outbreak that had killed Huayna Capac and Ninancuyuchi.

At the same time, the disruption of the world into which many had been born must have been psychologically devastating. General religious belief among Andean peoples acknowledged the arbitrary power of the gods, and the death of their emperor by such a mysterious disease must have been regarded as divine retribution for something he and they had done.

A PLANNED BREAK-UP?

Some sources indicate that Huayna Capac had planned to divide the empire among several sons. He was disturbed by a prophecy that the empire was ending and that he was the last of the Inca dynasty. He told his sons that Inti had informed him that the demise of the Inca would come with the arrival of powerful foreigners and that the priests had foretold all: a new moon had appeared with three halos, which they said represented the death of Inti, war among his descendants and the break-up of the empire. Some scholars even think that the Inca Empire was over-extended and would not have been able to sustain its unwieldy size – that it was effectively self-dividing by 1526.

Below: Sapa Inca Atahualpa, who challenged the heir designate, Huáscar, when their father Huayna Capac died. From an 18th-century 'Cuzco School' Inca genealogy.

PIZARRO'S CONQUEST

Pizarro's three expeditions (1524–5, 1526–7 and 1531–3) to north-west South America seemed to be the fulfilment of the priests' prophecy. He made his first contact with Inca subjects in 1526, when he encountered a balsa trading raft with two traders from the Inca subject port of Tumbes, laden with gold and silver objects and textiles. The traders described the cities and wealth of the empire to Pizarro.

CLASH OF CULTURES

When Francisco Pizarro began his final expedition, he carried in his head visions of the fabulous civilizations and riches of Mesoamerica. He also projected the confidence and superior attitude of Europeans of the 16th century towards other cultures. Although he undoubtedly appreciated the sophistication of the Inca

Empire when he saw it himself – how else could it have built the great cities and amassed the riches he saw? – he also held in contempt foreign peoples whose religious beliefs were regarded as heathen and whose political and military abilities were regarded as inferior. The irony is that the Incas, in many respects, felt the same about the peoples they had themselves only recently conquered. Both the Spaniards and the Incas held their peoples and cultures as the pinnacle of social, political and technological achievement. Their abiding philosophy was that they were destined and entitled to rule the known world.

MULTIPLE FACTORS

Despite the obvious disruption of the civil war, what really brought the Inca Empire to its knees? By the time Pizarro arrived on the borders of the empire, Atahualpa had won and was in the process of reconsolidating Inca administrative structure and institutions. The

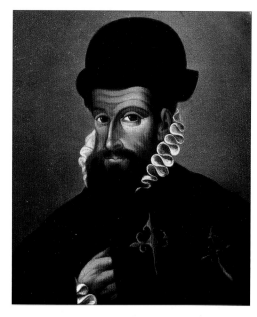

Above: Francisco Pizarro (1475–1541), Spanish foundling, illiterate pig herder, adventurer and conqueror of the Inca Empire.

empire was weakened, but Atahualpa still had his army, which was vastly superior in numbers to Pizarro's force.

The factors that ensured Pizarro's victory over the Inca are varied.

Despite their seemingly perfect world, in which everyone got what he or she needed, the imperial household was clearly becoming overburdened and demanding a large proportion of the empire's resources. There were also problems with the imperial succession: with so many potential heirs from multiple wives, there were bound to be court intrigues and contestations of legitimacy.

The empire was still expanding north when the Spaniards arrived, and their huge southern acquisitions beyond the Titicaca Basin were very recent. The peoples of many provinces simply bided their time through the civil war. Many must have resented their recent subjugation but were still in awe of Inca power and in fear of the strange events taking place.

The succession to the throne was not fully decided. Many Inca nobility still opposed Atahualpa even though he had

Below: Rebellious uprisings were dealt with severely by the Spaniards, shown in an execution scene by the Flemish Theodore de Bry in his Historia Americae *(1602).*

defeated Huáscar. When he occupied Cuzco, Atahualpa ordered the provincial governors and chief administrators to attend him in the capital. Many were of Huáscar's royal *panaca* lineage. Atahualpa committed acts of sacrilege by ordering them put to death, and, further, by ordering the burning of the mummy of Tupac Yupanqui, Huayna Capac's predecessor and ancestor of the *panaca*. These acts not only effectively eliminated potential claimants to the throne, but also broke the imperial line and contradicted the very concept of the Inca world, so fulfilling Huayna Capac's prophecy.

The coincidence of Huayna Capac's death by smallpox and the ensuing civil war can only be labelled a quirk of historical fate. What Pizarro did to seize the opportunity is, however, down to the audacity and character of the man himself and of his Spanish companions. He took advantage of the Inca's own road

Below: Pizarro demanded a room full of gold as ransom for Sapa Inca Atahualpa. This fanciful depiction includes un-Inca classical columns and a medieval chair.

Above: This modern interpretation of the Sapa Inca Atahualpa meeting Pizarro in 1532 in Cajamarca captures something of his alleged haughty nature and elevated importance.

system to move quickly into the heart of the empire, meeting with little resistance. Realizing the disruptive influence of the civil war, he was quick to exploit Atahualpa's hesitation to confront him. He also declared his intentions to be peaceful, possibly to ally himself with one side. He was astute enough to assess the Inca state of mind and to take advantage of their religious beliefs and the prediction of their demise. And he was simply bold and knew that at his age and at this stage of his 'career' the stakes were high and that he must not lose the opportunity.

He was right in most respects. The atrocious acts by Atahualpa against Inca world concepts left his subjects in a stupor. They had seen Atahualpa's hesitancy to challenge Pizarro and witnessed his weakness when captured and his orders to strip the empire of its wealth to ransom himself. They had underestimated the superiority of Spanish technology, misread Pizarro's motives and were unprepared for the psychological impact of ambush – a most un-Inca act. After the ambush and capture of Atahualpa, many finally rebelled, welcoming and joining the Spaniards to throw off the burdens of Inca rule.

DIVINE FATE

The psychological impact of the smallpox epidemic cannot be underestimated. During Huayna Capac's illness, traders from the northern borders reported to him the appearance of bearded strangers in strange ships and reminded him of his priests' prophecy of the end of the Incas. In the Andean belief in the arbitrary power of the gods, it was unambiguous that the disease was divine wrath. The appearance of people who were immune to it made them ready to accept the prophecy, divine approval of the newcomers and the fate of their civilization. Francisco Pizarro himself died a relatively young, supposedly rich, man, murdered by the hands of his own countrymen.

Finally, it must be said that reverence for their local landscape and many ancient beliefs endure today alongside Christian faith as proof of the quiet resilience of ordinary Andeans.

Below: Post-conquest rivalry among the Spanish conquistadors is exemplified in this unsympathetic caricature of Pizarro by 18th-century artist James Gillray.

CHAPTER TWO

FROM VILLAGES TO CITIES

The development of Andean civilization is divided by archaeologists into a series of defined time periods. This is for organizational convenience, for in reality such divisions are false because they are too rigid and because Andean ancient societies evolved continuously as they adapted to their times.

Through periods of climatic change, population increases and political upheavals, Andean peoples developed social, economic and technological structures and expertise. They slowly accumulated layers of social and political sophistication and religious complexity, moving from bands of hunter-gatherers through the more sedentary lifestyles of agriculturalists to the complicated lives of urban citizens.

As societies increased their ability to produce the essentials of life, more and more people were able to have jobs that were not linked with food production. In this way, specialists were able to increase in number and skill. True urbanism was achieved when the juxtaposition of political, bureaucratic and economic activities balanced and intervened between religious and domestic life. Technical skills and full-time specialization – in crafts or politics or religion – can be sustained only if the economic structure can support them, and the attainment of this balance is the hallmark of urban civilization. This chapter outlines the sweep of Andean prehistory from the first peopling of the continent to the Inca Empire.

Left: The sun temple ruins at the Inca royal estates at Rosaspata in the Vilcabamba Mountains, Peru.

THE FIRST ARRIVALS

People (modern *Homo sapiens*) migrated into the New World from the far north-eastern reaches of Asia during the final stages of the last great global Ice Age (the end of the Pleistocene Period), from at least 15,000 years ago. The archaeological evidence for this migration is scattered and comes from land sites in North, Central and South America. Geological evidence shows us that the world sea level at this time was lower by about 100m (330ft), because much water was still frozen in ice sheets and glaciers. A huge ice sheet covered most of the northern half of the North American continent, extending south from the Arctic.

MIGRATION ROUTES

The lower sea level created a land bridge across the Bering Strait, and the general chronological and geographical distribution of the evidence for the arrival and spread of hunter-gatherer peoples indicates they took this route into the New World. They followed an ice-free corridor that opened up in the western half of the continent between the Cordilleran and Laurentian (or Laurentide) ice sheets,

Below: A Moche moulded red-ware effigy jar, c.400AD. The face reveals 'typical' features of Andean peoples.

Above: Early migrants into South America encountered harsh environments such as the Atacama Desert of northern Chile.

migrating from the north-west to the south-east. As they found ice-free lands south of the ice fields, they spread east, west and south. They found the continent to have a vast larder of long-established animals and plants, most of them indigenously evolved species, and some large game animals (or their immediate ancestors) that had probably migrated from Asia during earlier breaks (interstadials) in the ice sheets – for example the Columbian mammoth, or American mastodon.

This conventional reconstruction of events has been challenged and modified in recent decades. It seems logical to assume that migration also took place by sea along a western coastal route. Island- and coastal-hopping in pursuit of sea mammals lacks direct evidence, which presumably lies beneath the water off the present coastlines. Another recent theory argues that there was also an earlier migration across the ice floes of the North Atlantic into north-eastern North America. This argument is based on conclusions about similarities between the European Solutrian lithic culture of south-western France, dated 22,000–16,500 years ago,

and the Clovis stone point tradition of North America, dated about 10,000 years ago. This theory is rigorously disputed.

MIGRATION GROUPS

Molecular biology, DNA and blood-group evidence shows that these New World immigrants descend from three or four distinct populations, revealing there were several incidents of migration into North America. Those peoples who continued into South America, however, descend from only one of these biological groups.

Below: An imaginative painting showing how the first migrants into the New World from north-east Asia followed game across the land bridge created across the Bering Strait during lowered sea levels in the late Ice Age.

The rate of migration is also a point of controversy and can only be guessed. Nevertheless, the earliest indisputable date for human occupation in South America comes from Monte Verde, southern Chile, about 14,850 years ago (averaged from more than a dozen radiocarbon dates), showing that the pace was rapid, or that early evidence from farther north remains to be found.

MONTE VERDE

At Monte Verde, a group of people lived for a season or two on the banks of a small creek. Eventually, their settlement was abandoned and covered by a peat layer deposited by the river. Their settlement comprised crude wooden-plank or log-floored pole- and hide-walled rectangular huts. There were at least 12 contiguous rooms or huts arranged in two parallel rows. Within them and around the site were found remains of wild potatoes and other plant remains, animal bones (including mastodon) and wooden and stone tools: wooden spears, digging sticks, three wooden mortars, stone scrapers (including three with wooden handles) and egg-sized pebbles, some grooved, believed to be sling and bolas stones. There were also clay-lined hearths for cooking and one human footprint preserved in the peat.

Separate from the dwellings was a single, 3 x 4m (10 x 13ft), Y-plan structure made of a sand-and-gravel floor, and two rows of wooden poles with hide walls forming the arms. The rear of the hut was

Left: Early hunter-gatherers left examples of their art on rock, as here in a depiction of a snake hunt in Zamora, Ecuador.

raised, and the open area between the arms had several clay-lined braziers and the remains of animal hides, burnt reeds, seeds and medicinal plants, including chewed leaves. Other hearths, piles of wood, artefacts, and plant and animal remains were scattered around the structure. Clearly this was a building for special purposes.

SCARCE EVIDENCE

Such rare preservation demonstrates the scarce nature of the evidence for early lithic cultures in the Andean Area. This Archaic or Lithic Period lasted down to about 7,000–5,000 years ago in different areas of the Andes. Lithic sites and surface artefacts have been found throughout South America, including Brazil, Argentina and Uruguay, and the tip of Tierra del Fuego. Finds of lithic artefacts and occupation remains become more widespread after about 7,000 years ago. The varied terrains occupied gave rise to different artefact styles, including adaptations to the mountain environments, where several fluted projectile point styles were used in hunting horse, sloth and other animals, and to several coastal traditions along the Pacific coast, where bone harpoons were used to hunt maritime mammals.

Below: An essential New World hunting tool – and later weapon in war – was the atl-atl. *Two hunters are poised to hurl their spears with* atl-atls *at vicuñas on a Nazca pot.*

PRECERAMIC VILLAGES

The persistence of lithic-using hunter-gatherer cultures varied in different regions of the Andean Area, and there are few hard facts about exactly where and how the domestication of plants and animals took place in the Andes and western coastal valleys. Increasing heavy exploitation and reliance on certain species appears to have led to plant tending, which, after many generations – both of human populations and of the plants themselves – led to modifications to enhance the species and its yield.

DOMESTICATION – THE THEORY

There are some tens of thousands of plants and animal species in South America, but less than 1 per cent of these have been domesticated. It is argued that in regions where a species thrives and is abundant in its natural environment there is little reason for humans to tend or otherwise try to manipulate it, since they can simply gather it as needed. However, in marginal areas of a species' habitat, there is a need to nurture it if there is to be

Below: Llamas provided many products for early peoples in South America. As well as hunted quarry, they soon became domesticated as herded flocks in the Altiplano.

sufficient for human use, especially if the population in an area is increasing. Species found outside their known native regions can thus be regarded as 'domesticated'.

There are changes in environmental conditions and climate over short distances within the Andean Area, especially with altitude change. Thus even small movements of a species into a new environment introduced human selection as well as natural selection. It is believed that constant 'experiments' of this nature by an increasing human population brought domestication to selected food crops and fixed human reliance on a small number of species. At first they were able to exploit these crops in naturally watered soils; later, in an extension of the experiment, they grew them in soils to which they could bring water through irrigation schemes.

Significantly, however, the earliest known domesticated plants come from Guitarrero Cave, northern Peru, from *c*.8000BC. Fibre-plant remains dominate the Guitarrero assemblage (used for sandals, clothing, cordage, bedding mats and mesh sacks), but there were also specimens of domesticated beans and chilli pepper, both *not* native to the region and therefore probably cultivated there.

Above: One of the earliest uses of clay was for unfired figurines, such as this model of a woman from the early Valdivian culture in Ecuador, c.3500–1500BC.

The increased reliability of selected cultivated food sources also made it possible for people to congregate in larger settlements and to remain there permanently, rather than having to move through the seasons to exploit food sources in their own native environments. Gradually, both in lowland coastal and highland valleys, the number and sizes of settlements grew.

LATE PRECERAMIC ECONOMICS

Three elements form the foundations of the economic developments that characterize the late Preceramic Period in Andean prehistory. These are: the intensive exploitation of maritime resources at coastal settlements; the use of floodplain irrigation in coastal valleys and rainfall agriculture in highland valleys, for early agriculture; and long-distance trade. The last of these elements established, from the earliest times of

Above: A painting from the Mollopunko caves, northern Peru, c.5000BC appears to show a llama being led or tethered with a rope, an indication of early semi-domestication.

permanent settlement, an Andean tradition of reciprocal exchange between highland and lowland communities.

The richness of maritime resources on the Pacific coast made it possible for coastal peoples to live in large settlements mostly supported by maritime food sources. Sites have deep middens of accumulated shellfish, crustacean, fish and sea mammal remains. Until the late Preceramic and into the Initial Period, grown foods were only a marginal part of the diet, but nevertheless included squash, beans, chillies and two introductions to the coast (potatoes and maize) by c.2000BC. Such is the scene at sites up and down the coast, such as Huaca Prieta and Salinas de Chao on the northern coast, Aspero and Piedra Parada on the central coastal, and El Paraíso and Otuma on the southern coast.

Such intense exploitation of maritime resources, however, would not have been possible without a source of cotton for nets and fishing line and gourds for floats. Both these plants are not native to coast environments, and were introduced from tropical regions to the east and north, where they were domesticated early on.

HIGHLAND CHANGES

Similar changes took place in the highlands. Annual precipitation of 5 to 6 months not only supported a rich natural flora but also appears to have provided hunter-gatherer peoples with several intermontane-valley species that became the staples of their diet: potatoes, maize and beans, and a host of other tubers, grains and legumes. There was also meat, including deer, vicuña and guanaco (which remained wild), and the llama, alpaca and guinea pig, all of which show cultural and anatomical signs of domestication by the end of the Preceramic Period.

Plant domestication was underway by 5000BC in the highlands. By about 3000BC most of the full range of food plants capable of being grown in highland valleys had been adopted. Similarly, the guinea pig was bred as a domestic meat source, although anatomical evidence at this early date is insufficient to determine how far true domestication had proceeded. The domestication of the llama and alpaca, herded on the grasslands of the Altiplano, took place gradually over 2,000 years and was complete by c.25,000BC.

Such was the scene at the beginning of the Initial Period at sites such as La Galgada and Huaricoto in the northern highlands, Kotosh and Shillacoto in the central highlands, and Ondores farther south.

Below: Fishing became another important ancient Andean economy. The Aymara still use traditional totora-reed boats to fish on Lake Titcaca on the border of Bolivia–Peru.

THE INITIAL PERIOD

Beginning *c*.2000BC in the Andean Area, the Initial Period was a time of tremendous technological advancements and accomplishments. First, there was a flowering of textile technique and art when the simpler techniques of fibre twining and looping began to be replaced by cloth woven on heddle looms; second, the first ceramics began to be made in the Andean Area; and third, there was growth in monumental architecture building.

WEAVERS AND POTTERS

The invention of weaving using a heddle loom enabled the mass production of cloth. It went hand in hand with developments

*Below: A terracotta figurine (*c.2300BC*) from the Valdivian culture of coastal Ecuador, some of the earliest pottery in the Andes.*

in farming and pastoralism. As the farming of greater areas of land produced increased yields in cotton, and the expansion of llama herding in upland regions increased the availability of wool, so the innovation from simpler techniques meant that more textiles could be produced by specialists.

The first ceramics in South America were made, from *c*.3200BC, in the extreme north of the Andean Area by the early farmers of Valdivia on the coast of Ecuador. Pottery of a slightly later date (*c*.3000BC) was produced outside the Andean Area by people at Puerto Hormiga, on the Caribbean coast of Colombia.

For both weaving and pottery making, labour became more concentrated and specialists became possible. The increase in large building projects also fostered the development of social organization that featured specialists in two fields: those who planned and built them, and those who ran them. As some members of society concentrated their skills in agricultural production, so increasing the agricultural yields achievable by fewer farmers, other people were able to devote more of their time to ceramic production and weaving.

SPECIALISTS

No doubt the bulk of the population was not particularly specialized, and the majority of people probably continued to spend most of their time in agriculture, herding and other subsistence pursuits. But the increasingly greater availability of food for less effort inevitably gave people more time to vary their daily lives and to pursue craft activities beyond the purely useful. As a result, forms and varieties of decoration increased and regional styles developed. Thematic motifs reflecting religious belief became incorporated into ceramics and textiles, and special pieces were made for burials.

Together with an increasingly sophisticated evolution in religious beliefs, these innovations and developments themselves

Above: Irrigation techniques using narrow channels to route water into fields, developed by the earliest farmers, continued to be used until Inca times, as here at Tipon, near Cuzco.

became interwoven, on the basis that ceramic production and decoration, textile styles and decoration, and architectural construction were never separate thematically. Religious motivation and the demonstration of religious themes were always incorporated into Andean technological production and architectural form.

PUBLIC ARCHITECTURE

Perhaps these reconfigurations of social structure and time management are most dramatically represented in the expansion of monumental architecture. The size and planning of monumental architecture mirrors religious concepts in mimicking the sacred landscape and in orientation to the sources of sacred waters. Form also reflects what are assumed to be beliefs in Mother Earth and Father Sky deities.

Two classic forms were developed: the platform mound and the sunken court. Platforms supported single or multiple rooms. Often the two forms, plus subsidiary platforms, were combined in complexes forming a U shape. These forms established the traditions that would prevail through the Initial Period and into the Early Horizon.

INLAND MIGRATION

Settlement patterns also changed. Increases in agricultural production were in part made possible by shifting settlement to areas with greater expanses of better-watered lands. The largest centres of population shifted systematically inland in the central and northern coasts of the

Below: Fertile flatland was at a premium in the mountain valleys, so extensive terracing was used to create thousands of narrow fields, as here in Colca Canyon, Peru.

Andean Area. Settlements along the shoreline were abandoned in favour of richer-soiled valley mouths and lower valleys, where river water was more accessible. Maritime resources were not abandoned, but the dependence on agricultural crops by these coastal populations brought important shifts in emphasis and must have had profound effects on the organization and scheduling of their daily lives. Where formerly they lived on the seafront and brought agricultural produce to their settlements, they now began to live in towns among their fields and to travel to the seaside to collect shellfish or embark on fishing and sea mammal hunts.

The reasons for these changes are debated. From the late Preceramic Period, coastal settlements that were predominantly reliant on maritime resources had also incorporated newly domesticated food crops into their economy. But they had been reliant on small satellite settlements

Above: An Inca farmer tapping an irrigation channel to water the maize crop in November (a dry month), depicted in Poma de Ayala's Nueva Corónica, *c.1615.*

in the lower river valleys for agricultural produce, which might imply at least a rudimentary kind of irrigation.

What began in the Initial Period, and what in fact partly defines the period, is the development of much more substantial irrigation works, tapping the rivers with channels to run water into the fields. One reason might have been population growth and consequent pressure on resources. It is certain, however, that the abundant maritime resources would have been able to support even larger populations than our present archaeological knowledge shows us. We also know that there were small environmental changes in the coastlines that left some settlements more isolated from the sea. But these shifts were gradual and subtle.

What seems the best explanation includes both these factors, plus social and economic relationships that had developed in rudimentary fashion in the late Preceramic Period simultaneously. A combination of changing dietary preferences, increased success in farming, socio-political rivalry to control the best resources, and shifting patterns of work as these agricultural 'discoveries' were made seems to be a more plausible cause for both changing settlement patterns and the artistic, architectural and religious enhancements of the Initial Period.

THE EARLY HORIZON

The Early Horizon is defined as a period of cultural cohesion across large regions of the Andean Area, comprising northern and southern spheres. These spheres were not mutually exclusive: there were relationships, trade and influence between their communities, maintaining already-developed Andean cultural traditions of long-distance trade between highlands and lowlands.

INITIAL PERIOD TRADITIONS

The Initial Period flowering in monumental architecture developed into several regional traditions, both coastal and highland, and served the first Andean religious cults. These developments formed the basis of much more widespread Early Horizon traditions.

The classic form was the U-shaped complex, comprising a central mound, wings forming a U, and sunken courts. Many platforms supported complexes of small adjoining or individual rooms. These forms established the traditions that prevailed throughout the Initial Period and into the Early Horizon.

Sunken courts (called *plazas hundidas*) were one tradition. They were usually part of a complex with platforms mounds, but could be on their own. A second tradition, called Kotosh, featured a one-roomed enclosure for intimate worship.

Two further traditions, Supe and El Paraíso, show a new order of magnitude and organization. Earlier ceremonial complexes are more modest in size and are usually associated with domestic remains, indicating that they were built by their local communities. Complexes of the Supe and El Paraíso traditions, however, are larger, more complex and varied, and lack evidence that they were surrounded by immediate residential populations. They appear to be the earliest complexes that were built and maintained as centres for religious worship for regions of communities. The El Paraíso U-shaped ceremonial centre is a representative example of such a complex, associated with irrigation agriculture and dominating the Rimac Valley on the central southern Peruvian coast. The largest U-shaped complex ever built was Sechín Alto in the Casma Valley.

At the same time, the Chiripa Tradition developed in the Titicaca Basin. This consisted of symmetrical arrangements of one-roomed buildings around a square sunken court atop a low platform. The type-site is Chiripa on the southern Titicaca lakeshore, with 16 buildings around its sunken court.

SOCIAL ORGANIZATION

The strong association of monumental architecture in ceremonial complexes serving regions and irrigation agriculture indicates that kinship relations between communities formed strong links. This was an important Initial Period/Early Horizon development that endured throughout the rest of Andean prehistory.

It seems likely that linked communities and shared religious traditions strengthened social systems of communal labour,

Left: Chavín de Huánta united Andean and coastal people in the name of religion – the flanking columns of the Black and White Portal of the New Temple show an eagle (female) and a hawk (male), early examples of duality.

Above: 20th-century archaeologists at work at Chiripa Pata, a pre-Tiwanaku site with a massive temple.

co-operative administration between communities of irrigation works and water rights, perhaps collective land ownership and entitlement to shared resources. Lineage groups were probably moiety-based (two intermarriageable family groups of a descent lineage) from this early period (defined by the *ayllu* in Inca times).

EARLY HORIZON CULTS
These coastal and southern ceremonial centres waned and were eventually abandoned in the early centuries of the 1st millennium BC. In their places arose even stronger, more widespread religious traditions. Two spheres of development can be identified: a northern sphere dominated by the site of Chavín de Huántar and its religious cult, and a southern sphere, slightly more diversified, but with strong religious cults called Pukará–Yaya-Mama in the Titicaca Basin and the Paracas Oculate Being along the southern coast.

CHAVÍN DE HUÁNTAR
With the abandonment of Sechín Alto and other coastal centres, the beliefs and administrative organization associated with U-shaped and sunken-court complexes endured in the highlands. The small, unimposing site of Chavín de Huántar took up the mantle of regional religious focus. Settlement began *c*.900BC at the confluence of the Mosna and Wacheksa rivers, a site apparently deliberately chosen to take advantage of access to western coasts, mountains and eastern

tropical lowlands. The Castillo temple was a classic U-shaped form, although the platform is not high. It endured about 700 years, including phases with an Old Temple and a New Temple, first with a circular sunken court and later with a square one. The ceremonial core was less than a tenth the size of Sechín Alto.

The Castillo appears to have been a cult centre and pilgrimage site for almost the entire Andean Area. Its success can be attributed to established long-distance trade, the spread of Chavín symbolism on portable objects and the integration of llama-herding with irrigation agriculture. While Yaya-Mama and Oculate Being imagery were confined to their respective southern spheres, Chavín's appeal cut across old social boundaries and regionalism, and its universality is demonstrated by the appearance of the Staff Deity as far south as Karwa on

Below: The Oculate Being in his human form, wearing a Paracas-style golden diadem and holding a trophy-headed snake.

Above: Ancestor worship as seen in a Paracas burial tomb containing mummy bundles wrapped around the elite person's body.

the Paracas Peninsula, and of Chavín symbolism on stone sculptures at Pacopampa and Kuntur Wasi in the northern highlands.

The spread of Chavín religious symbolism was extraordinary. Arising at the end of a drought period that caused abandonment of the coastal centres, it catered to coastal and mountain deities alike. Its religious symbolism embraced general concepts of dualism, and earthly and celestial deities represented on a succession of huge stone idols, as well as smaller objects with representations of the Staff Being as both male and female, a feline-serpentine image and a great cayman idol. It is significant that none of the animals or plants on Chavín's stone carvings is native to its highland location.

PUKARÁ AND PARACAS
As the importance of Chiripa waned, so Pukará, north of Lake Titicaca, and about a dozen other sites north and south of the lake, became centres for the Yaya-Mama Cult. Its symbolism was the duality of male and female figures carved on opposite sides of stone stelae. The cult flourished at the same time as Chavín through the middle centuries of the 1st millennium BC.

On the southern coast, the settlement of Paracas represents a third Early Horizon cult, with its extraordinarily rich cemeteries serving regional communities. The principal deity here was the Oculate Being, colourfully represented on textiles and pottery as a wide-eyed, flying sky deity.

THE EARLY INTERMEDIATE PERIOD

Chavín de Huántar was not the capital of a state, but rather a place of religious focus, and the cultural coherence that defines the Early Horizon was religion. While the inhabitants of other cult centres, such as Karwa, Kotosh, Huaricoto, Pacopampa and Kuntur Wasi, clearly felt religious allegiance to the Castillo temple, there is no evidence of political control at sites with Chavín Cult art. There is no identifiable state administrative architecture or other evidence of other than local regional community government and social arrangements.

THE END OF CHAVÍN

Although the demise of Chavín de Huántar and its cult was sudden, the reasons are obscure. Monumental construction in northern and central Peru came to an abrupt end in the 3rd century BC. The centuries either side of the Early Horizon–Early Intermediate Period were plagued by drought. Scholars attribute Chavín's end to an inability to maintain stability and the redistribution of resources during such stressful times.

Below: The capital of the Moche state featured a huge ceremonial centre, including the Huaca del Sol and, shown here, the Huaca de la Luna temple mounds.

Perhaps the length of its success was due to an acceptance of fate and to a focus on religious faith to counter hard times.

THRESHOLD OF URBANISM

Chavín de Huántar and its influence brought Andean civilization to the brink of urbanism, but lacked a truly urban appearance. Its economic life, including the support of craft specialists, was centred on its religion and ceremony.

The abrupt deflation of such strong cultic and artistic coherence brought social withdrawal. Hard times caused greater competition and many centres were abandoned, while others became impoverished. Squatters, for example, occupied the circular sunken plaza at Chavín de Huántar. There were population shifts to hilltop fortresses on both the coast and in the highlands.

With climatic improvement, the best lands were occupied and population increased. Highland peoples combined terraced and raised-field agriculture with mountain pastoralism, while desert coastal peoples built extensive irrigation systems to water the valley bottoms. But once the easily exploited lands were filled, competition was again inevitable. Intermittent periods of drought again punctuated the first few centuries AD.

Above: The Early Intermediate Period Kingdom of the Moche was the Andean Area's earliest state in northern coastal Peru, established through military conquest, exemplified by this effigy pot of a Moche war leader.

Unlike in the Initial Period and Early Horizon, Early Intermediate residential communities outnumbered purely ceremonial ones, and were larger. Although many settlements were fortified, often on hilltops and ridges, undefended settlements were the norm, and small villages filled the valley bottoms.

POLITICAL AND SOCIAL CHANGE

There was a shift from religious cultism to political rule by powerful elites. The political shift was from the powerful

Right: Nazca religious practice featured thousands of individual lines and ground figures – geoglyphs – across some 640 sq km (425 sq miles) of desert floor, forming ritual pathways, such as the famous hummingbird figure.

influence of priests to rule by *curacas* (a noble or kingly class distinguished by wealth and power) in the name of the gods. Ceremonial structures were built by the rulers, who marshalled the labour of their 'subjects'.

The civilizations of the Moche in the northern coastal valleys and of the Nazca in the southern coastal deserts demonstrate these changes most clearly. Both developed and flourished from the beginning of the 1st millennium to about AD700. Other nodes of political power were in the Rimac Valley of the central coast (the Lima culture) and several highland states.

INCREASE IN URBANISM

The settlements of these cultures are characterized not only by their greater size but also by the variation of their architecture. Ceremonial centres were still distinct, and sometimes separate, but they were now surrounded by or linked (twinned) with residential areas developed with regular planning. Buildings reflected activities, showing administrative,

craft specialization and domestic functions. Residence sizes and decoration reveal variations in wealth and status – the birth of socio-economic classes.

Religious overtones in philosophic outlook were still a driving force in people's day-to-day existence, and religious symbolism still dominated art, but the juxtaposition of political, bureaucratic and economic activities, and their intervention between religious and domestic life, form the complexity of parts that define urbanism. These developments were in place throughout the Andes by about AD500.

SPECIALIZATION

Each of these regions produced distinctive ceramics, metalwork and textiles. The renown of Moche craftsmanship rests especially in the quality and quantity of its metallurgists, whereas the potters and weavers of Nazca, where the desiccated conditions of the desert have preserved textiles in particular, possessed an expertise achievable only by specialization. Technical skill and full-time specialization are

Left: Contemporary to the Moche, the Nazca peoples of southern coastal Peru formed a loose confederation of states. Much wealth was represented by their exquisite, colourful textiles, such as this hat, especially associated with ancestor worship and burial.

hallmarks of urbanism. Such practices can be sustained only if the economic structure can support them. There was state sponsorship of crafts, and objects were commissioned by the elite and made specifically for occasions, such as elite burial.

Battle scenes are a frequent Nazca and Moche artistic theme. Particular to Moche culture was a state specialization in ritual combat. Selected boys – the job might even have been hereditary – were trained from an early age to participate in gladiatorial contests with religious overtones. Moche ceramics depict some of these individuals in series of portrait vessels that show them through their lives, revealing those who were successful enough to last until they became the sacrificial victims when their skills waned and they lost their contests.

Particular to Nazca were its ground drawings: animals, plants and geometric shapes outlined on the desert surface were ritual pathways, binding society with religious ceremony.

Representative of these developments are the cities of Moche surrounding the ceremonial mounds of Huaca del Sol and Huaca de la Luna, Gallinazo, Sipán, Pampa Grande and Pañamarca in the northern coastal valleys; Pachacamac and Maranga in the central coast; and the twinned Cahuachi and Ventilla cites in the Nazca Valley. In the northern highlands were Cajamarca, Marca Huamachuco, Recuay and Wilkawain; Huarpa to the south; and in the Altiplano, Omo and the rise of Tiwanaku.

THE MIDDLE HORIZON

The Middle Horizon is defined as a further period of increased unity across regions. Precedents had been set in the later Early Intermediate Period with the evolution of more secular political regimes, albeit of city-states ruling small territories. The difference is in the underlying reasons for cross-regional unity: in the Early Horizon it was religion, while in the Middle Horizon it was politics, economy and military conquest.

MOCHE AND NAZCA

The closest thing to a large area under single rule in the Early Intermediate Period was the Moche Kingdom in the northern coastal valleys. Even this state, however, was characterized by semi-independent rulers from one valley to the next. The Moche were a seafaring people who pursued conquest from one

Below: A kero *drinking cup in the form of an effigy vessel – a puma head – also with a stylized beast and many typical Tiwanaku angular motifs.*

Above: Pikillacta's substantial stone walls formed the regimented town plan of the Wari highland provincial capital near Cuzco.

valley to another by sea invasion, as generations of the sons of kings sought new territories when valleys risked becoming overcrowded. The Moche shifted their centre of power from south to north, from Moche in the Moche Valley to Sipán, and later to Pampa Grande, in the Lambayeque Valley, in the 5th–6th centuries AD. By contrast, the Nazca culture was characterized by what appears to be a loose grouping of city-states.

RISE OF EMPIRES

Moche power collapsed and the Nazca and highland city-states waned with the rise of two civilizations that effectively split the Andean Area between them. They were the Wari and the Tiwanaku. Both expanded through military conquest and colonization. Each had a recognized imperial capital: Huari in a south-central highland intermontane valley between the Huamanga and Huanta basins, and Tiwanku near the southern shores of Lake Titicaca.

From AD650 the political states established by these two civilizations raised the socio-political level of Andean civilization to a new degree of urbanism and state control that in their turn provided models for later powers such as the Chimú and the Inca.

Above: The Wari provincial town near Ayacyucho, Peru, shows modular, angular, slab-like stone wall architecture.

SHARED RELIGION, DIFFERENT POLITICS

Wari and Tiwanaku religious symbolism was largely similar. Their rulers and people worshipped the same mountain gods, although they represented them in different media. The focus was on the Staff Deity, represented in imagery similar to that of the Chavín Cult, and which had been so widespread in the Early Horizon. Both Wari and Tiwanaku built in megalithic styles, but large-scale stone statuary was a particular Tiwanaku artistic and religious expression (and one that impressed the Incas centuries later, because it survived, standing silently among the ruins of the ancient city when Inca armies entered the Titicaca Basin).

The differing origins of the two capitals reflect different bases of each empire's power. Tiwanaku had been settled much earlier and had been part of the Early Horizon cult of Pukará–Yaya-Mama. It was thus steeped in religious cult practice. By about AD200 major building was under way and the city soon became the focus of Titicaca Basin religion and power. Tiwanaku representation of the Staff Deity on the Gateway of the Sun can be viewed as taking up the mantle of Chavín de Huántar.

Huari's rise was much later. A small settlement began to expand rapidly at the end of the 5th century AD. Within 100

Above: Tiwanaku, capital of the southern Andean Middle Horizon empire, features numerous enclosed ceremonial compounds at the heart of the city, including the Semi-Subterranean Temple Court, whose walls have sculptured decapitated heads and whose steps lead up to the gateway to the Kalasasaya sacred compound.

Below: The so-called 'monk', one of several colossal stone statues at Tiwanaku, stands in the Kalasasaya sacred compound.

years it was a dominant political power in the south-central highlands and began to expand through military conquest.

ADMINISTRATION AND COLONIZATION

Both empires grew as they took and exercised control of larger areas, each expanding north and south. They met at the La Raya Pass south of Cuzco, and in the upper Moquegua Valley, and there established their borders, under the watchful eyes of Wari garrisons at Pikillacta and Cerro Baúl. There seems to be less evidence of overt militarism at Tiwanaku, while the regimentation of Wari sites appears more martial. Evidence of violence is present in both, however, including stone sculptures of decapitated heads.

In both regimes, their provincial cities and holdings were linked by roads and trade connections, indicating the control of resources. One of Wari's earliest established provincial capitals, Viracochapampa, was 700km (435 miles) north, indicating direct control. This Wari infrastructure was later rejuvenated and improved by the Incas.

Wari expansion appears to have been stimulated by economic tension. To stay in power, Wari rulers needed to secure and control resources. They established deliberate agricultural colonies, such as Jincamocco and Azángaros, and provincial capitals at Viracochapampa and Pikillacta, all in the mid-7th century AD.

Tiwanaku colonization was different. It had a strong agricultural base in the Titicaca Basin, and within this heartland its control was direct. Farther afield control was through trade, for example to San Pedro de Atacama 700km (435 miles) south in northern Chile. Actual colonization by Tiwanaku was closer to home – for example at Omo, west, in the lowland Moquegua Valley, and in the Cochabamba Valley, east, in both cases in sparsely occupied areas – to secure resources they could not grow in the Titicaca Basin.

PATTERNS OF CONTINUITY

These alternative configurations of state organization reflect the path of Andean civilization nicely. The Chavín Cult had introduced widespread religious cohesion despite relative autonomy in local political and social arrangements. Fragmentation of cohesion in the Early Intermediate Period had more to do with the cessation of Chavín influence than with changes in local-level politics or day-to-day life.

The different beginnings and evolutions of these two Middle Horizon empires reflect both elements: imperial state political control from a military base in the case of Wari, similar to Moche expansion, and the centralized cult status and economic basis of Tiwanaku control.

THE LATE INTERMEDIATE PERIOD

Wari and Tiwanaku powers waned swiftly in the final century of the 1st millennium AD. Reasons for the collapse of states are forever debated, but it seems that both empires may have become over-extended. As they colonized areas to secure resources, they no doubt raised resentment among some of their subjects. Abandonment of many of their provincial cities appears to have been sudden.

There is also climatic evidence. Data in cores taken from the Quelccaya icecap and from Lake Titicaca sediments show that rainfall decreased from c.AD950 and introduced a new, prolonged period of drought. The lake level dropped several metres (yards) and effectively ended the easy irrigation of raised-field agriculture.

Increased tension, failed crops, social unrest and the breakdown of trade links – all must have contributed to the swift declines of both capitals and their provincial settlements.

FRAGMENTATION AND WARFARE

Once again Andean societies withdrew into their local economies. As had been the case in the Early Intermediate Period, political and macro-social regimes fragmented into city-states, and for roughly the next 400 years local leaders seized power.

Left: A gold and jade repoussé decorated kero *drinking cup, with Staff Being-like imagery of a Sicán Lord, shows the richness of elite north coastal Peru Lambayeque tableware.*

Above: A Chimú finely woven textile exhibits repeated figures wearing elaborate 'ceremonial' headgear and large earrings, plus felines.

With the Late Intermediate Period we come to the threshold of recorded history. Spanish chroniclers, transcribing the histories narrated to them by Inca and other native informants in the early 16th century, describe the period just preceding the rise of the Inca Empire as one of intense warfare between competing 'tribes' or ethnic groups. Strong, warlike leaders were called *sinchis* and they built many hilltop fortifications called pukarás, as shown in the archaeological record.

The Inca themselves, in their battles with neighbours in the Cuzco Valley, were participants towards the end of these developments, and indeed their second ruler (12th century) was named Sinchi Roca.

COASTAL STATES

Settlement patterns changed again as people isolated themselves in their local mountain valleys, often living in, or building for retreating to, fortresses overlooking their agricultural lands. Cultural initiatives and the focus of political power returned to the coast with the abandonment of Huari and Tiwanaku.

The traces of Moche culture that lingered in the northern coastal valleys were picked up by leaders living there, perhaps inspired by the visible ruins of the great Moche platform mounds. Following only brief domination by Wari, the Lambayeque-Sicán rulers established a capital at Batán Grande in the La Leche Valley. Like the Moche, they were renowned for their superb metallurgy, known from the royal burials discovered in the capital. Their kingdom was eventually incorporated by the Chimú.

On the central coast, several city-states arose as focuses of local power: the Chancay, Ichma, Cerro Azul and Chincha, all throwing off Wari rule. And the long-established city and pilgrimage oracle of Pachacamac in the Lurin Valley enjoyed a building boom that established it as the premier religious centre along the coast and to the stressed inland communities as well.

Above: A characteristic Chimú polished black effigy vessel or stirrup-spout bottle features a seated priest or elite person seated at a 'throne'.

On the southern coast, the Ica emerged to rule in the Nazca region, while farther south the Chiribaya people emerged from the power vacuum left when the Tiwanaku abandoned the Moquegua Valley.

Highland peoples are less identifiable archaeologically, although many tribal names were recorded from Inca informants. This is partly because they left no substantial legacy of monumental architecture or art, as did their coastal counterparts, before the Incas conquered the highlands.

To combat reduced rainfall and thus a fall in agricultural productivity, people were forced to concentrate on their local situation and to move to higher, moister elevations and into the wetter, eastern Cordillera. Increased use of terracing was necessary to grow sufficient crops. Competition fostered class separations, as the *chullpa* stone tower burials of the elite show.

Around Lake Titicaca, internecine rivalry resulted in the formation of a loose kingdom of seven confederated capitals or city-states.

CULTURAL DIVERGENCE

Fragmentation was not only political and social. Although art and architecture shared basic technology, approaches and subject matter, inheriting long developments in Andean civilization, the styles became regional: Sicán, Chimú, Chancay, Ica and Chiribaya. Architecture continued to be 'additive', and textiles, ceramics and metalwork mass-produced, standardized and prone to the use of repetitive patterns. Nevertheless, there were distinctive regional styles that can be identified with ethnic groups, both in the highlands and on the coast, the latter

Below: Labyrinthine corridors, compounds and storage rooms are formed within poured-mud, sculpted walls at the Chimú capital of Chan Chan.

Above: The poured-mud walls of Huaca el Dragón, a Chimú temple near the capital Chan Chan has rows of bas-relief warriors surrounding the 'rainbow' sculpture.

area being better documented archaeologically thanks to a return by Andeans, perhaps in their troubled times, to religion. Interestingly, the styles of these coastal peoples are recognized in the offerings they brought to the oracle city of Pachacamac.

Increased emphasis on social hierarchies and the accumulation of wealth by social class and individuals were the result of competition for resources. Elites show a voracious appetite for collecting and hoarding luxury goods. Regimented social control became a hallmark of late Andean social structure.

CHIMÚ

Around AD900 a new city was founded opposite the great Huaca del Sol and de la Luna. This was Chan Chan of the Chimú, which became the capital of the largest kingdom ever seen in the area, subsuming Lambayeque-Sicán culture after invasion c.1350. Its rulers, like the Moche, looked to the sea rather than to the highlands for their economic base. They invaded the adjacent valleys and eventually held the peoples of the valleys as far south as Lima in a tightly controlled administrative state. Before their conquest by the Inca, the rulers of Chimú collected huge wealth and created an imperial bureaucracy within their sprawling capital.

49

THE LATE HORIZON

The conquest of the Chimú Kingdom by the Incas in *c.*1462–70 marks a final episode of the Late Intermediate Period, mainly as a convenient historical date. Other scholars prefer to use 1438, the traditional date for the defeat of the Chancas by Pachacuti, the tenth Inca ruler of Cuzco.

By definition, the Late Horizon was a time of uniformity after a period of diversity. The meteoric rise of the Incas spans the two periods, and a date at which this was achieved to mark the end of the 'period' and the beginning of the 'horizon' is a moot point.

Below: An Inca-style geometric design embellishes this silver dish – tableware for nobles or for ritual offerings – from Ica in the Inca western suyu-quarter of Cuntisuyu.

LEGACY

The legacy of political and social fragmentation in the Late Intermediate Period highland valleys aided the Incas when they began to expand beyond the Cuzco Valley. Their forces frequently met weak or no organized opposition from people in farming communities still recovering from times of drought.

In the central sierra, however, they met stiff resistance from the highland group of city-states called Wanka (or Huanca), in the region of Lake Junin and the Mantaro, Tarma and Chanchamayo rivers. These peoples were primarily llama herders and had not adopted intensive maize agriculture until *c.*AD1000. They built fortified hilltop towns and resisted the Inca armies fiercely, no doubt

Above: Typical Inca close-fitting stonework in a trapezoidal, double-recessed niche with capstone arch in a Cuzco wall.

helped by their knowledge of the terrain. In the end, however, they were defeated by Pachacuti.

The Inca regime was the inheritor of all that came before it. Characteristic of the Inca Empire, above all else, is the Incas' incorporation of the political, social, religious and military cultures of their predecessors. The special talent of the Incas was in their expansion and intensification of these Andean practices.

ACHIEVEMENT

The Incas conquered an empire, albeit fleetingly, that was the largest territory in the world *c.*1530. Over the peoples of their empire they imposed, again only fleetingly, a level of uniformity that had never before existed in the Andean world. The uniformity, however, was less in art and architecture than in the organization of people's activities and social structure. They built extensively, but did not replace existing settlements by rebuilding them, and encouraged local crafts to continue, organizing the produce into their highly controlled economic bureaucracy.

Inca genius lay in their abilities to organize, incorporate and manipulate, and in their engineering. Inca power was expressed especially in their stonework: they rebuilt Cuzco and built provincial administrative capitals with walls of perfectly fitted monolithic blocks.

The Incas rejuvenated, improved and expanded on the roads and way stations built by the Wari and Tiwanaku throughout the central and southern highlands. And they incorporated many Wari outposts. The Incas' own road network comprised more than 33,000km (20,000 miles) of routes linking their capitals and fortresses. Likewise they exploited, extended and increased the terracing and raised-field systems of highland and Altiplano peoples, and expanded irrigation systems, in the never-ending need to increase production for expanding populations.

From the Wari they also copied the practice of relocating people to exploit resources. And they adopted the Wari use

Below: An Inca chicha *'beer' jar with typical geometric decoration.*

of the *quipu*, the string and knot system that served as a means of recording administrative essentials and statistics.

Above: To feed the huge population of the empire, the Incas made extensive terracing wherever possible to extend agricultural lands, as here at Moray near Cuzco.

THE INCA MESSAGE

The Incas approached politics, social organization and art in terms of standardization and set units. While Inca standard shapes and patterns were imposed, aspects such as different colours marked regional and tribal identities.

In contrast to the intricate technology and exquisite beauty in much of the art and architecture of pre-Inca cultures, Inca art is more geometrically regular and less iconographic. Things Inca seem minimalist and utilitarian by contrast to the art of other Andean cultures. (Sadly, most Inca metalwork and sculpture, and much of their textiles and ceramics, were destroyed by the Spaniards.) Spreading their culture over newly conquered peoples was more to do with giving an impression of imposing power than imposing a new or complex symbolism. The sheer amount and bulk of Inca architecture and its road system, all of which served its bureaucratic organization and social control, was the message.

Even Inca religion was practical. In the late 14th and 15th centuries they increasingly pushed the imperial state cult of Inti, emphasizing that the Sapa Inca was the direct descendant of the sun. But they also left local religious belief in place, absorbed local belief into their own and continuously rewrote their history or left it vague with multiple versions and interpretations, to incorporate regional beliefs into the state mythology. The Incas did not challenge the obvious importance and influence of the Pachacamac oracle, but insisted on adding to the importance of the ancient pilgrimage city by building a temple to Inti there to add to the city's importance within the empire.

The imposition of Inca control was total in principal, but practical in application. As long as tribute in produced goods was paid and the labour tax obligation met, the imperial household was satisfied. They reciprocated, albeit non-symmetrically, with the redistribution of their subjects' produce such that all received what they needed.

The Incas generally improved the lives of their subjects and brought peace after their conquests, which was surely better than the continual warfare and competition over resources, both access to them and control over their movements and distribution, that had gone before.

CHAPTER THREE

BUILDING AN EMPIRE

The Inca Empire was forged in under 100 years, but the cultural development that preceded it took over 2,000 years. The Incas are recognizable archaeologically by a distinctive artefact assemblage, artistic expressions and architecture by *c*.AD1200.

The widespread exchange of traded items and ideas from the Preceramic and Initial periods coincided with the beginnings of monumental architecture at coastal and highland sites. The occurrence of common commodities, exotic items and artistic imagery reveals the beginnings of pan-Andean concepts that endured for the rest of Andean prehistory up to Inca times.

The Inca Empire brought a unity never before seen in the Andes over such a large area. Inca unity, however, was not based on imposed cultural uniformity. The Incas encouraged the regional diversity among their subjects, utilizing their cultural and artistic differences. At the same time, they controlled their movements, regulated the distribution of goods and wealth within an imperial economy, and imposed an all-inclusive religious conformity. They left their subjects in no doubt as to who was in control, and that resisting imperial rule was futile.

Four major concepts underlay the ancient Andean worldview: 'collectivity', 'reciprocity', 'transformation' and 'essence'. The names are words applied by modern anthropologists, but the ideas they represent would have been instantly recognizable to ancient Andeans. These ideas underpin everything from the most overarching institutions to the smallest details in ancient Andean art.

Left: When the Incas took over the pilgrimage shrine at Pachacamac, they built their own Temple of the Moon there.

CULTURAL UNITY (COLLECTIVITY)

The concept of collectivity is the idea of corporate thinking. From early times, Andean cultures thought in co-operative terms. People undertook activities that required collective and co-operative efforts, and the organization necessary to achieve agreed goals. Collectivity's underlying basis is that the group is more important than the individual, and in turn that the individual is looked after by the group. The idea involved every member of society in a web of responsibility to contribute to the whole.

Early tools were probably made by most individuals, or within small family groups. As populations increased and lived together in greater numbers, however, those more skilled in different materials or tasks could specialize in them. Specialists could then exchange each other's products or efforts.

By the time of the Inca Empire, and its immediate predecessors, the presence of specialists is known from descriptions of Inca society and its kinship and state structures. Archaeological evidence of similar structures and products in earlier cultures shows Inca culture was the culmination of many earlier developments.

Above and below: Religious themes and economic interdependence spread across vast areas from high lakeland valleys such as the Lake of the Incas (above) to dry landscapes such as the Atacama Desert (below).

This recognition of signs of collective thinking means that the general idea of these cultural features can be projected back to the earliest times. Certainly, many imperial constructs of Wari and Tiwanaku civilization are evident in Inca culture.

COTTON GROWING

The earliest coastal fishing villages reliant on marine resources fostered communities in which each member contributed a part. Fishermen and shore collectors required both intra- and inter-group co-operation, and the collections of both groups were pooled and redistributed within the community.

Cotton fibre was essential for tools for exploiting the marine environment – for nets, line, traps and bags – as well as for clothing and other household items. An increased reliance on cotton, and presumably a growing population needing clothes, led to it eventually being grown as a crop, so securing more control over supply.

Preceramic Period fishing villages dotted along the Pacific coast cultivated fertile flatlands in nearby lower river valleys to grow cotton for use in textiles. Similarly, the domestication of food plants and a few animals also fostered, and must have been achieved originally by, communal effort in highland valleys. Whether common or individual, fields needed watering and tending, and the development of irrigation systems and terracing to exploit more land required collective labour and co-operative use.

Above: This Chancay textile shows several characteristics of unity: figures in a Staff Being-like stance, angular geometric patterns and a monkey figure from the rainforest.

CO-OPERATION IN ADVERSITY

Although marine resources and agricultural production could be abundant, variations in climate and weather could bring cycles of drought or El Niño events, creating times of acute stress. In addition, the general harshness of some Andean Area environments – drought and unproductive years, desert and mountain terrains, each of which had limitations as to what resources were available or could be grown there – caused chronic stress. The people had to adapt socially to meet the demands of these environmental conditions.

The storage and redistribution of food within a community, so evident in Inca society, developed much earlier to supply individual specialists with food and drink, while they supplied artistic, political and religious expertise. Communal co-operation produced sustenance, tools and clothing, and sustained spiritual needs.

MONUMENTAL CO-OPERATION

The construction of monumental architecture in the Preceramic and Initial periods shows corporate effort on another level. It reveals the existence of inequality within the social structure. When large groups of people undertake communal, labour-intensive projects, some individuals need to organize and direct the enterprise. Such leaders need to exercise power among individuals, and thus authority becomes unequally distributed.

Further, the isolated nature of early monumental complexes – for they were not residential places – suggests that they served the towns and villages of the regions around them. Their shapes – pyramidal platforms supporting holy buildings and enclosed spaces clearly meant for crowd assembly – and the artefacts associated with them – figurines and stone sculptures regarded as idols representing deities, the finest ceramics and textiles, and imported items – show that their purpose was for the worship of religious ideas and accepted deities.

Taken together, these features reveal the birth of corporate thinking within and between communities, and of religious concepts that shared widespread acceptance.

ARTISTIC COLLECTIVITY

Collectivity in ancient Andean art can be seen through a certain emphasis on sameness. The limited number of basic ceramic forms, for example, shows conservatism through time, despite details of cultural style that make it possible to identify places and times of manufacture. In all artistic media there is a de-emphasis on portraiture and individual historical detail in favour of an emphasis on common types.

Deities and the general portrayal of them reveals a similar conservatism in the use of Staff Deity figures, and serpentine, feline, severed-head and other imagery. Both real-life and supernatural imagery focuses on roles rather than on individuals, portraying acts and practices rather than specific events linked to known individuals. The detailed decorations on ceramics, textiles and metalwork often concentrate on continuous and repetitive patterning and are often abstract.

Below: The ancient shape of the kero *cup changed little from Nazca to Inca times, and geometric designs perpetuated over millennia.*

TRADE AND MUTUAL OBLIGATION

A second fundamental Andean concept, reciprocity, becomes apparent early in cultures in their long-distance trade and the care taken in burials. It is linked to collectivity in a form of partnership in social structure, economy and art.

OBSIDIAN AND WOOD

Economically, reciprocity involves the exchange of resources. Exotic materials from the highlands were sought by lowland peoples, and vice versa. The exchange of goods is well demonstrated, both archaeologically and in Inca history.

Archaeological evidence shows that reciprocal exchange between lowlands and highlands began in the Preceramic Period, starting an economic pattern that prevailed throughout Andean prehistory. The full range of early highland–lowland exchange is still unknown, but from earliest times it included raw materials, food and finished artefacts. For example, obsidian (a natural volcanic glass used to make cutting blades, scrapers and projectile points) occurs only in highland areas above 4,000m (13,000ft), yet small quantities were found at most Preceramic and Initial Period coastal sites

(e.g. Ancón, Asia, Aspero and Otuma) from at least 3000BC. The closest obsidian source to Aspero is Quispisisa in the south-central Peruvian highlands, 385km (240 miles) to the south-east.

Similarly, wooden thresholds in doorways at coastal Río Seco were made from trees that grow in the highlands between 1,450m and 3,000m (4,800ft and 10,000ft). The strength of these exchange links is revealed by the fact that neither obsidian nor wood is essential in a coastal economy, yet they were preferred to local materials.

FROM FISH TO FEATHERS

Fish and salt were naturally lacking in the carbohydrate-dominated diet of highland peoples, yet not only are Pacific fish bones and shells found at all Preceramic highland sites with monumental public architecture, but there is also evidence of a trade in salt with coastal sites, where salt-making was carried out in large stone mortars.

Importation of thorny oyster shells both to highland and coastal sites reveals that exotic items from the fringes of the Andean Area were also sought. So, too, does the trade in tropical rainforest bird feathers, imported to highland and coastal sites across the Andes.

Maize, first domesticated in lowland river valleys, was soon found to grow from virtually sea level to 3,350m (more than 10,000ft), and so was added to the highland cuisine. Reciprocally, the discovery of potatoes, oca and ulluco (two other tubers) at some fishing villages reveals that coastal peoples also sought highland foods.

CLOTH AND IDEAS

Manufactured goods were also exchanged. Llama wool from the pampas grasslands was sought by coastal Early Horizon

Left: A Paracas culture wool poncho depicts characteristic Paracas repetitious figures, in wool imported from the llama-herding peoples of the Altiplano.

Paracas and later Nazca weavers to work with alongside cotton for mummy burial wraps. Farther north, cloth at Initial Period Galgada bears designs similar to those on textiles from coastal Huaca Prieta and Asia. And a distinctive stone bead with convex faces on both sides and two parallel drilled holes has been found at both coastal (e.g. Aspero and Bandurria) and highland (e.g. La Galgada and Huaritcoto) sites.

The exchange of objects and commodities also brought the spread of ideas. Similar artistic imagery is the principal sign of this, but the spread of maize and potato growing is another, if more mundane, example. Serpentine, feline, crustacean and avian imagery was used on gourds, ceramics and textiles from the earliest times, spreading among coastal and highland peoples and enduring through time.

KIN AND SOCIAL OBLIGATION

At the same time, the links brought by contact and trade forged personal and communal alliances. Intermarriage was

Below: A Chancay feather headdress exemplifies trade for colourful tropical birds from the eastern rainforests across the Andes to the western coasts.

Above: The early development of weaving led to trade in cotton and llama wool between lowlands and highlands (woman weaving, as depicted by Poma de Ayala, c.1615).

bound to take place, and the resultant blood ties between highland and lowland groups brought reciprocal obligations.

Kinship relations became extremely important in Andean society and are documented for the Late Intermediate Period and Late Horizon as the *ayllu* system. In Inca society the *ayllu* defined a community bound by kinship and territory. The *ayllu* social unit was also defined in political, ritual and economic terms: it could be a band of people or faction, or a state or ethnic group.

The operative force was that each member of the *ayllu* owed other members of the group, and the group as a whole, obligations in labour, food and goods, protection and social ceremony in exchanges to assure the group's cohesion and continuity. These blood relationships extended across generations.

Each *ayllu* could trace its origins back to founding ancestors, and mummified ancestors were honoured and regarded as sacred to the point of including them in community religious ritual and involving them in community decisions. On ceremonial occasions and religious festivals, the mummies were fed and consulted on agricultural and social matters.

Furthermore, there were obligatory relationships between individuals and *ayllus*, on the one

hand, and the state on the other. In Inca times this was demonstrated by the *mit'a* taxation system, a binding agreement of expected produce or labour delivered or performed by *ayllu* members for the state (in the Inca case, for the emperor and imperial household) and for the state religious organization. This dual structure meant that *ayllu* members had to co-operate in selecting some of their members to perform labours for the state, while other members performed tasks within the *ayllu*, including tasks that would have been undertaken by the missing members while on *mit'a* service.

Below: Preservation of the dead by mummification and wrapping in multiple layers of woven textiles, began the practice of ancestor worship that endured from Chinchorros and Paracas to Inca times.

LIVING IN A TRIPARTITE WORLD

Like collectivity and reciprocity, transformation and essence are also related concepts.

LEVELS OF EXISTENCE

Ancient Andeans regarded the universe and existence as consisting of multiple levels. The Inca tripartite realms of living world, world above and world below described by Spanish writers recorded a belief that began in the Preceramic and Initial periods and was shown in temple architecture. Platform mounds, temple rooms and enclosed spaces and sunken courtyards are facsimiles of this conceptual world: sky gods and earth goddesses are symbolized by pyramids and sunken enclosures. The world in which humans encounter and interact with the gods comprises the temples and ceremonial courts and plazas. All levels connected and interacted. Each was vital to the existence of the other two.

TRANSFORMATION

It is thought that processions through temple buildings were symbolic movements from the realm of the womb (the sunken courtyard) to the realm of the sky atop the platform. From the platform, or within an exclusive temple, priests were able to interact with the gods on behalf of the people, transforming the will of the gods to the world of the Earth.

Much Initial Period sculpture appears to show priestly or shamanic transformation in another way, too. As well as being a conduit between the gods and living people, shamanic trance, achieved with the aid of hallucinogenic substances, made priests vehicles between the different levels of the Andean world.

At Preceramic Huaca Prieta, a kind of transformation can be seen in the textile image of two crabs, linked by their tails on one side, and the other halves of whose tails transform into serpents. But it is in the Initial Period that Andean artisans began to

Above: Transformation is implied by the scarification and feline-like nose of this stone trophy head from Chavín de Huántar, and by its presumably drug-induced stare.

show humans in states of transformation. A mud sculpture at Moxeke depicts a caped priest emanating snakes, and painted adobe friezes at Garagay appear to depict transformation from human into insect. Condor markings on the faces of the Mina Perdida fibre figurines provide another example.

JAGUARS AND STONE WARRIORS

One of the most graphic depictions of transformation, however, is at Early Horizon Chavín de Huántar, after which sculptures and ceramic modelling frequently show humans in states of trance or midway between human and beast. At Chavín de Huántar, transformation from human to jaguar is shown in a series of sculptured stone heads on the walls of the New Temple. Other human-to-animal transformations were worked into Paracas and Nazca textiles.

The importance of the concept carried through to Inca times. At the moment of near defeat by the Chanca (traditionally dated 1438), Pachacuti Inca Yupanqui

Left: This clay model of a Moche priest in a state of prayer with joined hands (note the reciprocal hands on his headpiece) appears to be in a state of trance, probably induced by ritual chanting and drugs.

called upon field stones for help, where-upon the stones transformed themselves into warriors to secure Inca victory, then changed back. Ever after, the stones were honoured as a sacred *huaca*.

ESSENCE

Uniting the concepts of collectivity, duality and transformation, essence embodied Andean preference for 'symbolic reality' over appearance. Symbolism represented reality, even if hidden by outward appearance. It was less important for an image to be seen than for it to exist for its own sake. Whether or not it was being seen, an object existed, and, more importantly, what it represented also existed.

This idea was extended to the dismissal of the need for a human audience in some religious rituals. These took place in the

Above: The sunken court of the New Temple at Chavín de Huántar continued the tradition of large enclosures for worshippers in front of temple platforms, on which priests performed religious ceremonies.

Below: Shamans were important figures in cultures through the Andean Area, depicted here in clay by Bahía culture (c.500BC–AD500), Manabi in Ecuador.

intimate confines of exclusive temples or in hidden chambers within temple mounds, enabling priests to control what the mass of people in the plaza witnessed. Thus, what the priests said or interpreted was the essence of what it was necessary for the common populace to know. And such practices simultaneously under-scored religious control and the idea that humans formed only one part in the Andean worldview.

With exceptions in Moche art, there was little recognition of individuals; rather, even where individuals were depicted, the essence of the depiction was the action performed by the person. Individuals were only a part in the whole and were subservient to the theme of the work.

SYMBOLIC CHARACTERIZATION

The paramount importance of symbolism was that it enabled Andean craftsmen to represent the character of a deity or religious concept with features that were commonly recognized. This imagery then spread through different religious cults and endured for great periods of time. So, although cultural styles are distinguishable in different Andean areas, and from different periods of history, many common feline, avian, serpentine, arachnid,

plant and other symbols and features continued to be used from the Early to the Late Horizon.

Essence explains why Andean potters used moulds to make thousands of identical pieces, mostly restricted to a handful of shapes; why metallurgists sometimes painted over the metal, or hid base metals beneath gilding or plate; why elite individuals had their tombs filled with products made primarily for their eventual inhumation; and why weavers executed such elaborate patterns that the subject became illegible but remained true to its supernatural subject matter.

The transformation of procession along Nazca lines, too, retained the essence of its making, for it was not necessary to see the figure in its entirety at once – only to experience the symbolism and meaning of the procession. Essence also explains the seclusion of some idols within hidden chambers while others were on public display. Control of the symbolism was in the hands of the priests.

THE ANDEAN WORLDVIEW

Concepts of universality, continuity through life and death, and a cosmic cycle were all encompassed in the Andean worldview. The development of such views in some ways mirrors the actual evolution of Andean civilization.

BIRTH OF STATES

Changes in Andean society through 'horizons' and 'periods' reflect the nature of these developments through time periods characterized by cycles of greater and less political unity. Periods of political fragmentation were followed by times of political unity, then were replaced in turn by renewed fragmentation. Throughout these periods of waxing and waning political unification and break-up, however, there were certain universal developments that persisted or endured despite the political organization.

Religious concepts that developed in the Initial Period and the Early Horizon continued through centuries and millennia,

Below: Inca religion focused increasingly on the supremacy of the sun, Inti, and Viracocha. When the Incas conquered Pachacamac, they incorporated the shrine into their state religion, but demonstrated their authority by building their own Temple of the Sun there.

and formed a backbone of fundamental and universal concepts for Andean pre-Hispanic cultural development. Social structures involving relations between kinship groups and between highland and lowland peoples continued and provided a stabilizing structure that enabled society to continue at local levels, whoever ruled.

A NATURAL ANALOGUE

Nature itself seemed to comply, and perhaps suggested the idea of cycles to Andean minds. Andean peoples, even as they expanded and refined their levels of social and political organization, remained close to the landscape. This closeness is reflected in the ways in which they moulded the landscape with their irrigation systems and terracing, carved boulders into shapes mimicking the land, and regarded springs, rivers and stone formations as sacred *huacas*.

Life on the land was a repetitious cycle from one generation to another. The germination, growth and death of plants and animals and their coincidence with the seasons formed a backdrop for Andean religious philosophy. The analogy of the cycle of life from an encased, moist plant seed, to a tender young shoot, then a sturdy stem yielding its fruits, to the failing stalk

Above: Coya Mama, representing the moon, married her brother Maco Capac. 18th-century 'Cuzco School' genealogy of Inca emperors.

and, finally, withering plant seems obvious. The seasons and periodic occurrence of drought and floods, as El Niño events altered the Andean weather patterns, provided yet another analogy.

This relationship between ancient Andeans and their philosophical outlook can be called 'ecological'. Because they

Left: The Sillustani chullpas *near Puno, Lake Titicaca, were repeatedly re-opened for new mummy burials by the elite of the 13th-century Collao state.*

The long-lived oracle site of Pachacamac on the Peruvian coast represents another legendary constancy. Named after the worship of the coastal creator god, the pilgrimage centre endured for more than a thousand years, into the Late Horizon, and its ruins remain a sacred site today.

By contrast, in the ancient north coastal kingdom of Lambayeque-Sicán, Fempellec, twelfth in the dynastic succession founded by Naymlap, attempted to remove the sacred idol of Yampalec from its temple to another city. He was thwarted and executed by his priests in order to maintain political and religious continuity.

Below: Lloque Yupanqui, legendary 12th or 13th-century third Inca emperor and direct descendant in the ayllu *kinship founded by Manca Capac, depicted in an 18th-century 'Cuzco School' genealogy of Inca emperors.*

perceived their environment as sacred, they believed they were on Earth not to exploit it, but rather to enjoy its benefits through the grace of the gods. Andeans did not see themselves as the centre or focus of the world, but only as one group among all living things – including animals, plants and the stars. It was through the concessions and indulgence of the gods, who are universal and constant, that people were able to use their fellow living beings in life.

CONSCIOUS CONTINUITY

The cyclical nature and renewal of life represented continuity itself. Conscious political and social actions and decisions by Andean peoples and leaders also reflect this concept.

Ancestor worship, which appears to have begun as early as the Chinchorros and La Paloma peoples some 6,000 years ago, continued in the selection of special individuals and the attempts to bury them in a way that preserved their essence and linked them to the present. By the Late Intermediate Period and Late Horizon, the regular re-opening of *chullpas* in the Titicaca region to bring out the dead, and the special storage and inclusion of *mallquis* mummies in Chimú and Inca ceremony, had brought the association into physical presence.

The *ayllu* kinship structure and requirements of reciprocity strengthen continuity because both giver and receiver know what is required and what can be expected. Based on the worship of *ayllu* ancestors, the Inca imperial succession exemplifies the idea of continuity in being, theoretically, decided according to accepted precedence and formula.

Both the foundation of the Inca state and its succession were grounded in the legendary band of brother and sister founders, premier among whom was Manco Capac, who became first emperor. In theory, each subsequent Inca emperor was a direct descendant of Manco and his sister-wife Mama Ocllo. Significantly, at a crucial moment in Inca history, Yupanqui, son of Viracocha (eighth Inca emperor), defeated the Chanca, who threatened to conquer Cuzco when Viracocha fled the city, and took the name Pachacuti (literally 'revolution' or 'turning over or around'). The Incas themselves thus recognized both continuity of rulership and a cycle of change when Pachacuti began his reign after his father, named after the creator god, had admitted defeat. The god Viracocha, however, remained supreme in the Inca pantheon.

RELIGIOUS CONTINUITY

Perhaps the most obvious indication of Andean continuity is shown in the evolution of its religion, and is prominently visible in its art and architecture.

EARLY TRADITIONS

Early ceremonial centres, and the development of religious traditions at coastal U-shaped structures, and as complex clusters of rooms and temples on platforms in southern highland regions, show prescient Andean religious focus. They also demonstrate the establishment of architectural forms that remained in use throughout pre-Hispanic Andean civilization.

Likewise the serpentine, feline, avian and arachnid imagery so prominent in early ceramics, murals and sculpture continued to flourish regardless of political power structures. It seems that Andean consistency was lodged in its religion and expressed through artistic imagery.

CHAVÍN

The most celebrated and long-lived religious cult of pre-Hispanic Andean civilization was that of Pachacamac. The model of the Pachacamac Cult is used to characterize the Chavín Cult of the Early Horizon.

Chavín de Huántar, a relatively small U-shaped ceremonial centre established in the late Initial Period, appears unprepossessing compared to many much

Below: The long-lived pilgrimage shrine of Pachacamac, centred on the temple mound and oracle of the supreme god Pachacamac.

Above: The New Temple – the deliberately located ceremonial site of Chavín de Huántar – began the Andean tradition of universal religion and pilgrimage shrines.

larger earlier and contemporary U-shaped ceremonial complexes. Its location, however, appears to have been deliberately chosen to command routes between coastal and mountain valleys.

Chavín's success and longevity are indisputably shown by the complexity of its temples and the expense devoted to their enlargement. The New Temple, built from c.500BC, more than doubled the size of the original complex and incorporated the older parts rather than abandoning them. A second temple was built, forming a larger U-shape, and a second sunken court, this time rectangular rather than circular. The complex plazas were capable of holding 1,500 worshippers, and there is evidence that the accommodations for priests and cult artisans increased in number and area.

The spread of the cult was through its religious imagery rather than by imitating its architecture, for no such complex, labyrinthine temple interior was built anywhere else. During the half millennium from c.500BC, Chavín feline imagery spread throughout the northern and central Andes and as far south as Karwa near Paracas in the southern coastal deserts.

Chavín's principal deities formed the core of what must have been a widespread, uniform religion that transcended local political arrangements. The Staff Being became a universal image of divinity and could be either male or female. Jaguar and cayman imagery on Chavín de Huántar's monumental stone architecture and statuary reveal the reach of Chavín interests and influence, for both jaguars and caymans are rainforest animals.

Chavín's sculptural style provides the main signs of the spread of the cult, as shown by portable objects produced by its temple craftsmen and copied locally. It is fundamentally representational, employing conventions that were intentionally mystified. The principal image of the deities was reduced to a series of straight and curved lines and scrolls, and animals were portrayed in formal poses with only essential details – a process termed 'idealization'.

Above: The ritual, sunken enclosure of the Kalasasaya Temple at Tiwanaku provided a large, confined area where worshippers gathered for religious ceremonies.

The intricacy of Chavín temple architecture provided a sense of convention, unity and mystery. There was ritual use of water, an upper platform in the Lanzón idol's chamber that enabled priests to hide and act as the voice of the oracle, and a secret interior passage that permitted priests to emerge suddenly from 'nowhere' on the terrace above the Black and White Portal façade to address the crowds in the plaza.

This combination of idealized imagery and intricate construction presents a series of religious metaphors whose deep meanings were understood only by the initiated. The archaeologist John Rowe likens Chavín's visual metaphors to the literary metaphors used in Old Norse poetry. In both, 'kennings' are direct substitutes whose meaning must be learned. In use they provide mystery and unintelligibility, the understanding of which only priests can provide.

PACHACAMAC

The cult of Pachacamac was so important and powerful that its influence has survived even the colonial conversion to Christianity. Native Andeans to this day travel to the ancient site to make offerings to Pachacamac (the creator) and to Pacha Mama (earth mother). No other Andean site played such a significant role for such a long time.

The widespread influence of the Pachacamac Cult probably dates back to about 1000AD, although the site was founded some time in the 1st century AD and soon became locally influential. Inca and early colonial sources describe it in detail, revealing its longevity and acknowledging its importance and power.

The principal monuments from this period were constructed by the Ichma, who united the Lurín and Rimac valleys of the central coast. Fifteen terraced adobe platforms were raised, with great ramps leading to their summits, along the city's two main streets, running north–south and east–west.

Walls and cell-like rooms surrounded each platform compound, which provided the settings for pilgrim accommodation, public feasting and public ritual preceding consultations of the Pachacamac oracle.

UNIFYING POWERS

We know that Pachacamac was feared because the god was believed to control earthquakes. It is reasoned that Chavín deities' powers lay in control of the weather: rainfall, thunder, lightning, hail, frost and drought.

Both Chavín's and Pachacamc's influence was primarily religious. It was the power of their cults that united people throughout the Andes. The political spin was provided by the Wari and later by the Incas, who each conquered Pachacamac and used its religious prestige to enhance their imperial powers.

Below: The New Temple at Chavín de Huántar hid a labyrinth of inner rooms, and a secret stair used by priests so they could suddenly 'appear' on top of the temple.

SOCIAL AND POLITICAL EVOLUTION

Ancient Andean civilization increased in social and political complexity through time. Bands of hunter-gatherers undoubtedly had leaders, and tasks must have been divided among band members, probably partly along gender lines.

SOCIAL HIERARCHY

From the Preceramic and Initial periods, religious architecture, differential burial treatment and the importation of exotic items reveal important differences in social hierarchy. Possession of special items enhanced social prestige, increasing an individual's power and influence. Two early examples occurred at La Galgada: a single salt crystal was placed beneath the head of the female in an early burial; and a bed of large salt crystals beneath a layer of charcoal formed the base of two later Galgada burials.

Special treatment after death continued throughout Andean prehistory as ancestor worship increased in elaborateness. By the Late Horizon, mummies were regularly included in social occasions and every community had its ancestor mummies.

Below: Burial practices of the Qullasuyus as depicted in Poma de Ayala's Nueva Corónica, *c.1615.*

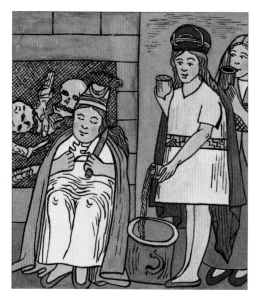

Above: Establishment of colonies and provincial capitals was an essential part of empire building and control, as exemplified by the regimented streets of the Wari provincial capital at Pikillacta.

CONSTRUCTIVE LEADERSHIP

Monumental architecture requires co-operation among large numbers of people, and directors. The association of differential burial and increasingly complex religious symbolism with ceremonial centres implies the emergence of rulers.

The spread of religious influence throughout large areas, especially from the Early Horizon Chavín Cult, shows the importance of inclusion, though inevitably the power of decision-making became the prerogative of some individuals over others.

In the Early Intermediate Period, coastal state organization was manifested in the Moche state and in the Nazca confederation of city-states. Individual highland city-states flourished, with shifting alliances, until greater unification came in the Middle Horizon with the rise of the Wari and Tiwanaku empires.

RELIGION AND POLITICS

Long-distance trade increased in volume and range through time, bringing tension as well as co-operation and reciprocity.

Tracking the spread of architectural, ceramic and other artefact styles helps us to trace cultural influences. The growth of the Wari and Tiwanaku empires is revealed by the presence of their distinctive ceramics and architecture as they conquered other peoples and built colonizing settlements. Wari outposts included Pikillacta, Viracochapampa, Jincamocco and Azángaros, and Wari pottery appeared at Pachacamac on the coast; a Tiwanaku lowland colony was established at Omo.

Politics and religion were never fully separate. Elaborate Paracas and Nazca burial bundles of important individuals included the cult trappings of trophy heads, while the Moche Sipán Lord burials included the costume of religious ceremonial leaders. The Inca emperor was the representative, perhaps even the incarnation, of Inti, the sun god.

INCLUSION

Organizational structures combined Andean economy, religion, society and politics alongside the unifying cultural and artistic concepts of collectivity, reciprocity, transformation and essence. The goals of Andean social and political arrangements were to secure basic stability and relative prosperity for all, guided by religious belief.

Andean civilization became grounded in state-like institutions (organized groups from across the social divisions working with understood rules of conduct); common beliefs – with powers of interpretation vested in a formal priesthood; state regulation of output; trade and the redistribution of wealth according to accepted social divisions; and state sponsorship of crafts and artistic production.

Inca inclusion of the gods of their subjects reveals the strength of Andean desire for continuity, as does their admiration for and imitation of earlier imperial structures, especially Tiwanaku and Wari. Admiring the ruins of Tiwanaku, they recognized the city and islands of the lake as sacred. They incorporated the ancient city and its beliefs into the imperial state religion, making Tiwanaku and Titicaca the womb of the universe. The official storyline became that the ancestral Inca founders came from there, sanctioned by Viracocha.

Below: The ostentatious regalia of the Moche Lord Sipán burial demonstrates the wealth accumulated by Moche rulers and the skill of their state-controlled craftsmen.

Similarly, Inca inclusiveness adopted Pachacamac, both the deity and the sacred city. Typical of Inca mastery, they acknowledged Pachacamac's antiquity, but took over the shrine, making their supremacy clear by building a temple to Inti next to the ancient temple. To them, it was important to maintain continuity, but also to demonstrate who was in charge.

INCA EXPANSION AND DECLINE

The nature of Inca expansion shows these elements in action. As one tribal state among several in the Cuzco Valley, early Inca expansion required warfare.

As their power grew, however, they employed a variety of strategies. Military conquest continued – for example, the growth of alliances in the Lucre Basin powerful enough to rival their confederation resulted in Inca conquest. In other cases, subjugation was achieved through marriage alliance, or long-established cultural affiliation with the Inca led to gradual political incorporation by the more powerful Inca. Inca interest was in control, not destruction.

An interesting twist is that at the arrival of Spaniards equally resolved on control, sibling rivalry over the imperial succession threatened its continuity internally alongside external threat.

Above: The Spaniards built their Church of Santo Domingo on the shrine of the Inca Temple of the Sun in Cuzco.

A final contributing factor in the demise of the Incas and Andean civilization was biological – the unintentional biological warfare of smallpox. From a population of about nine million in 1533, the native Andean population had been reduced to 500,000 by the early 17th century.

EVERYDAY SURVIVALS

Many fundamental Andean patterns survived the Spanish Conquest. Dietary staples remain maize, potatoes and tubers, as do ways of growing, processing and storing them. Rural markets remain essential. Weaving remains important in Andean economy, both for local consumption and, now, for tourism. Patterns persist, including designs and garments that identify regions. Pottery is still made with coils and moulds, although the art is being slowly eroded by use of plastic containers.

Finally, rural 'vernacular' architecture itself has changed little: cane thatching and adobe mud bricks are still in use, retaining ancient practical solutions to local environments.

STRUCTURE OF EMPIRE

The nature of the Inca Empire was grounded in the slowly evolving principles of earlier imperial states, especially those of Wari, Tiwanaku and Chimú. But although many Inca achievements were based on existing institutions and technologies, it was the scale of their empire that distinguished it.

INCREASE AND ELABORATION
Not only was the Inca Empire the largest in area of any empire in the New World, covering even more territory than the contemporary imperial Aztec state of Mesoamerica, but large size and scale also characterized everything the Incas did. Urban organization, buildings of large, dressed stone blocks without mortar, extensive road building, terracing and landscaping, and their complex administration and organization of textile and ceramic production and metallurgy were all sized and scaled to impress. Inca enterprises often utilized what other states had established or achieved, but they always elaborated, expanded or increased it.

Right: An Inca provincial administrator with his staff of office, depicted in Poma de Ayala's Nueva Corónica, *c.1615.*

The Incas defined their empire through physical structures imposed on the lands of their conquered provinces. The great emperors Pachacuti, Tupac Yupanqui and Huayna Capac – who expanded the empire beyond the confines of the Cuzco Valley – negotiated settlements with their subjects for the right to build roads, way stations and cities. Before embarking on military conquest, they professed friendship along with veiled threats, offering rich gifts to local rulers and the prospect of economic benefits through Inca administration. If such negotiations failed, however, Inca armies could be raised quickly and their well-organized supply systems enabled them to maintain standing armies at great distances from the capital. Inca repute was cumulative – the power and strength of organization in subject territories made the threat of conquest if non-coercive agreements failed all the more persuasive.

DIVERSITY ACCEPTED
While imposing their social regimentation, taxation system, laws and overall rule on conquered peoples, the Incas accepted the diversity of local customs. They incorporated local religious cults and deities into the state pantheon, while insisting on the overarching superiority of Inti and Viracocha. They imposed no dress codes, but allowed regional costumes to distinguish subjects and give them a sense of identity. Although Quechua was the language of administration, and became prestigious to use, they made no attempts to suppress local languages.

EFFECT ON ORDINARY SUBJECTS
The effects of the Inca Empire on ordinary lives were undoubtedly substantial, yet daily routines must have changed little.

Left: Forming the head of the crouching puma in the plan of Inca imperial Cuzco, the Sacsahuaman Temple to Inti, the sun, and fortress-weapons store emphasizes the power of Inca religion and state.

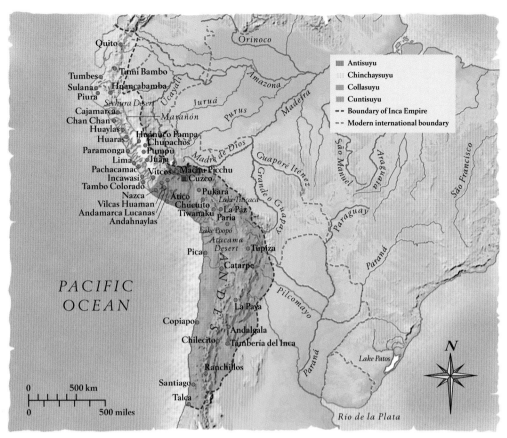

The changes were in emphasis and organization. To an ordinary subject, loyalty must have remained primarily to one's local officials. The systemization of work and the channelling of state quotas into its tripartite application (to the imperial household, the state religious establishment and the people) probably differed little in kind to the burdens of life that existed before incorporation into the empire.

Inca strength was in their brilliant and systematic organization of these matters, and in the powers of their ability to persuade populations to accept this organization, and to see the benefits it could have in times when environmental conditions and drought cycles adversely affected production, but when the state stores could then be drawn upon to redistribute goods.

Below: Inca architecture advertised Inca power, as here at the imperial palace and estate of Huayna Capac at Quispihuanca in the Urubamba Valley near Cuzco.

CITIES FOR STABILITY

The Late Intermediate Period was a time of political fragmentation in the highlands, although as Inca expansion began, Chimú continued the Moche and Lambayeque-Sicán succession on the north-west coast. Highland conflict punctuated the centuries from 1100 into the 15th century as El Niño weather events and consequent adverse environmental conditions led to competition for resources. The rise of the Inca Empire and its infrastructure offered resolution to this situation. Inca cities were established in response both to unsettled conditions and to the diversity of landscapes and cultures. The Incas established cities where they did not exist, to lay the foundations for rule, or altered and imposed their cultural stamp on existing cities to achieve the same result.

Their cities established a stage for pageant, spectacle and the display of wealth and power designed to win over their subjects. As ever in Andean civilization, reciprocity underlay this process, for it was a bargain. Not only was it necessary (to avoid military conquest) to gain the hearts and minds of the people, in other words their consent, but it was also

*Above: Map of the Inca Empire (*Tahuantinsuyu*), showing the four quarters (*suyus*) of the empire and major Inca towns and cities.*

an offer to fill their stomachs through an 'equitable' redistribution of life's necessities. People were accustomed to supporting the religious establishment, for it was an integral part of their worldview. They were also used to elite members of society – royal households and local rulers – having more. The Incas, however, offered to add stability and protection to what had been a more unstable arrangement, in return for loyalty and submission to an institutionalized labour tax (the *mit'a*).

The very name of the Inca Empire incorporates a subtlety that reveals the Andean concept of essence. Tahuantinsuyu means 'the four parts'. It was made up of a confederation of alliances, with varying degrees of loyalty, achieved through persuasion, military conquest and kinship ties through arranged marriages. The empire itself was relatively short-lived and, after decades of continuous expansion, had reached a state of civil war when the Spaniards arrived.

CHAPTER FOUR

THE WORLD OF WORK

Work in general in the ancient Andean world was primarily a continuous routine. Tasks were repetitive and linked to the succession of the seasons.

Much of our information about the economy of the Andean world comes from the ethnohistorical record of the Incas. For pre-Inca times, including the civilizations of the Nazca, Moche, Chimú, Wari, Tiwanaku and Sicán peoples, there is an increasing body of archaeological evidence, which gives us a great amount of detail, particularly about ancient technology. The nature of monumental architecture, and even of domestic architecture, helps to project much of what we know about Inca culture into the past, particularly concerning matters of religious worship. This evidence shows us where pre-Inca cultures differed as well as enabling us to deduce that many practices were similar in pre-Inca societies.

For example, the nature of trade and agriculture in Andean civilization as early as the Initial Period indicates that forms of social organization involving kinship relationships and the divisions of society were developed very early. Similarly, religious concepts and the roles of priests and shamans endured through the centuries.

Inca culture, although distinct, inherited a long legacy of ancient developments. Inca emperors and their administrators adopted and often adapted to local conditions within the confines of their own regimented organization of administration, taxation and social regimentation.

Left: State-supported craftspeople produced exquisite textiles, such as this Chimú nobleman's tunic with its long-billed birds.

CIVIL ADMINISTRATION

We know almost no detail about exactly how pre-Inca states organized society. There were buildings clearly for religious and administrative functions, including the storage and redistribution of goods. Usually the two 'institutions' were inseparable or closely linked, and there were specialists who governed or advised the ruler and others who were priests.

BEFORE THE INCAS

From at least the Early Intermediate Period on there were states, such as the Moche Kingdom of the north-west coastal valleys. The legendary Naymlap, the conquering king following the southern Moche collapse, had a court retinue listing numerous officials: 'Preparer of the Way', 'Blower of the Shell Trumpet', 'Master of the Litter and Throne', 'Royal Cook', 'Royal Cellarer', 'Maker of Feather Garments', 'Steward of Facepaint' and 'Master of the Bath'.

Not until the Chimú Kingdom (Later Intermediate Period) and the Inca Empire (Late Horizon) do we have any records of how states were organized.

SUYUS AND PROVINCES

The Inca Empire was divided into four quarters, called *suyus*, around Cuzco. These were divided into more than 80 provinces, each with a governor. If a conquered population was large,

such as the Chimú, it was designated as a single province, while smaller groups were amalgamated to form provinces. Groups of people were also moved from one province to another to induce loyalty to the empire or as punishment for rebellion.

In theory, each province had about 20,000 households, the basic unit of Andean society (comprising several nuclear families and several generations of related kin). The state bureaucracy was organized from the province downwards, to designate the proportions of land for imperial/state, religious and common use, to collect and distribute tribute, to regulate the *mit'a* tax system, to apply the law and administer justice, and to keep the peace.

THE ADMINISTRATIVE PYRAMID

The Inca emperor was the pinnacle of the administrative pyramid. Immediately below him were four *apos* (officials) in charge of the four *suyus*. *Apos* were close advisers to the emperor, and usually relatives. A governor of each province reported to the *apo* of its *suyu*. Provincial governors were usually Incas, but local chiefs were also used, especially in lower ranks of the administration.

Each province of 20,000 households was divided into administrative units on a decimal system. Two government officials

Above: A richly painted wooden Inca kero drinking cup showing a house and farmers with foot-ploughs and large storage jars.

called *curacas*, each in charge of 10,000 households, reported to the governor. Each *curaca* directed five lower-ranking *curacas*, each in charge of 1,000 households; each 1,000-household *curaca* directed two *curacas* of 500 households; and, finally, each 500-household *curaca* governed five 100-household *curacas*.

The *curacas*' main responsibility was to administer the *mit'a* labour tax – to make sure that the correct number of men turned up to work Inca lands, on building projects, serve in the army, work as a craftsman or various other Inca jobs. They also needed to make sure the burden

Left: Luxurious ornaments, such as these Moche gold earrings with lapis lazuli and shell inlay depicting Moche warriors, would have been worn only by rulers and nobles.

was equitably distributed among the household *ayllus* so that none was left with too few male workers. *Curacas* also collected the state tribute and saw to its delivery into state storehouses. They allocated lands to the households (on an annual basis as household constituencies changed). Lastly, *curacas* administered Inca law. Rewards came if all was done well; punishment if not.

SOCIAL CONTROL

Mitimaes (Quechua for 'foreigners') were people brought into a newly conquered territory to replace part of the indigenous population, and conquered subjects moved to the original homeland of the new settlers. They were groups of people forcibly resettled apart from their homelands.

The practice was used in order to exercise demographic and social control, and for economic reorganization. By resettling groups of people within the empire, the Incas could redistribute

Below: A native provincial administrator confiscates a llama as tribute, depicted in Poma de Ayala's Nueva Corónica, *c.1615 – the elderly owner claims that he is not subject to tribute.*

Right: The legendary northern coastal conqueror and ruler Naymlap, who maintained a large entourage of court officials, was depicted on numerous tumi *ceremonial knives, as in this gold Chimú example.*

labour and the commodities grown and produced by different groups, while also mixing together peoples' notions of geographic identity and religious/mythological concepts.

It served two purposes. By shifting people from their place of birth, the Incas exercised control over their destiny. It provided access to new geographical zones and enabled increased production in others. For example, moving a conquered group from a herding zone to a maize-growing zone increased the land available for imperial llama herds and simultaneously provided the workers to enable increased production in the maize-growing zone.

Such a move also helped to maintain control. Rebellious people removed from their homeland weakened both the group moved and their own or neighbouring populations left behind. Equally, moved now to live among loyal subjects, they were less likely to cause trouble. In practice, *mitimaes* moves often involved both purposes, as a loyal group was exchanged for a troublesome one, thus securing the province and continuing its production.

Given Andean reverence for the landscape, removal to an alien place must have had a huge psychological impact. The transplanted group probably had a part of its *ayllu* kinship relations severed from those left behind and was forced to live among strangers whom they could not trust, away from their local deities and sacred *huacas*.

The practice also combined details in the creation myth, such that a pan-Andean/pan-Inca version was propagated.

The result bolstered and legitimized Inca claims of a right to rule – as a 'chosen' people whose divine ruler had sanction by descent from the sun god Inti or from the creator god Viracocha. The term was even used in the creation myth, when Con Tici Viracocha ordered the two survivors of the great flood, thrown up on land at Tiwanaku, to remain there as *mitimaes*.

KINSHIP TIES

The foundation of Inca society rested in kinship relations. The rules and ties of kinship were so well established by Inca times that they appear to represent the result of a long development of social and cultural relationships that began in the earliest Andean cultures. The integration of highland–lowland relationships, and the exchange of products locally and regionally, required that several economic tasks be done simultaneously.

The minimum unit that could accomplish such a balance is, theoretically, a married couple. Yet even with children old enough to help, the requirements of farming, housing, water-collecting, herding, hunting and domestic chores cannot be as efficiently accomplished by a nuclear family as they can be by a larger group. It is arguable that this led to the development of strong kinship ties within larger groups of people to distribute labour better, and to established obligations that each member of the group understood.

Above: A structure of multi-generational kinship obligations developed from early times in ancient Andean culture – Manabí terracotta models of women and children, Ecuador.

AYLLU AND MOIETY

When the Spaniards arrived, Inca society was highly structured and involved a hierarchical arrangement of kinship relationships and obligations called *ayllu*. *Ayllu* comprised both community-bound kinship and territorial 'ownership'. As a social unit, it was defined in terms of economic, political and religious cohesion. As a kinship structure, *ayllu* was based on blood and marital relationships. Each *ayllu* was related back to an accepted common ancestor, a 'founder'. A single *ayllu* could comprise a band, a faction, an ethnic group or even a state.

An idealized extended kinship chart would begin at the *ayllu* level, starting with its founder or founding ancestors. Members of the *ayllu* were grouped into two halves, known by the anthropological

living descendants   living descendants

LINEAGES

SUYUS

hurin   hanan   hurin   hanan

MOIETIES

AYLLUS

founding ancestor   founding ancestor

Left: Diagram of the Inca (and earlier) ayllu kinship structure, showing relationships from the founding ancestors through moiety divisions to living descendants of two ayllu collectives. There is a founding ancestor for each of many thousands of ayllus; each lineage group descends from the two moieties of that same ayllu.

term 'moiety'. In the Late Horizon, the Incas called the two moieties *hanan* (upper group) and *hurin* (lower group), and the peoples of each town and province were thus paired.

AN ORGANIZATIONAL CHARTER

The next grouping (or 'tie') was the *suyu*. The *suyu* was the land division assigned to a man and his family (a household), and in Inca times was also used as the fourfold division of the Inca Empire. The lineage of the *suyu* and their descendants comprised the immediate living members of the *ayllu*. In Andean belief, however, physical death was regarded as only one stage or state of being. The dead were equal participants in 'life' through

Below: The family unit was the basis of Andean society – ceramic models of a man, woman and child from the Negativo Carchi people of Ecuador.

ancestor worship, so the mummified remains of ancestors continued to be included in the social structure through ritual.

Ayllu was, therefore, not simply the organization of a group of people, property, and goods and possessions, but rather an organizational charter of relationships and obligations that enabled the tasks and problems of daily work and existence to be shared. Individually it provided a sense of belonging for *each* member and collectively it provided for the security of *all* members.

Ayllu members were not all equal, however. There were individual leaders, although their authority was limited within the obligations of the kinship arrangement. Leadership and greater authority, and indeed nobility, were hereditary. At birth an individual became ranked by his or her genealogical proximity to their *ayllu*, moiety, *suyu* and lineage founders. He or she inherited reciprocal relationships: obligations to and claims upon other members of their *ayllu* for rights, farm and pasture land, water, labour and other collective assets.

EVOLUTION OF *AYLLU*

The argument for the development of *ayllu* at an early date is twofold, based on evidence for social and economic evolution. For economic reasons, the first hunter-gatherer bands entering the Andean Area would have been small groups. Many individuals in a group would be blood-related, but there is no reason to suppose that bands did not meet and intermarry, so establishing kinship relations between groups.

In maritime Andean society, rich marine resources enabled large groups

Above: Both men and women worked in the fields – the Cocha Runa, or First Age peoples, ancestors of the Incas depicted in Poma de Ayala's Nueva Corónica, *c.1615.*

of people to live sedentary lives in seaside villages. Likewise, as plant domestication developed from the selection and tending of, first, wild plants then semi-wild plants and finally domesticated crops, people led more sedentary lives and gathered in large village settlements. Increases in food yield, aided by developments in irrigation, terraces and raised-field agriculture, enabled larger settlements, social specialization and increasingly complex social interactions. Co-operation between individuals and groups involved mutual obligations and, eventually, 'rules' to govern those obligations.

The second part of the argument is that the exchange of products and ideas across geographical zones, as shown in archaeological findings, inevitably included the movement of people from valley to valley and between highlands and lowlands. It seems equally inevitable, therefore, that there would have been intermarriage among people of different zones. These associations were presumably freely entered into in times of peace. Competition for resources, bringing warfare and conquest, would no doubt have resulted in forced unions as well, either by capture and rape or as a result of peace negotiations. Either way, blood relations and kinship ties would be established.

TAXATION AND LABOUR

The fundamental Andean 'capital' was labour. Kinship obligations were enshrined in reciprocity: acceptance that something rendered required a return of equal kind or value, called *mit'a* (Quechua) and *ayni* (Aymara). The concept applied both to *ayllu* relationships and the relationship between the Inca state and its subjects. Like *ayllu*, the concept was of pre-Inca origin; Chimú society was similarly arranged.

Mit'a and *ayni* gave each household access to more labour than it could muster from its own members. *Ayllu* obligations from brothers, sisters, their children, in-laws, nieces and nephews were available for labour exchange under reciprocal obligations, enabling everything from house building to canal construction and maintenance, farming and herding to be achieved. For example, farming tasks were done by *ayllu* teams, plot by household plot. Sometimes repayment was in equal value rather than in kind, such as food for labour. The Incas formalized the *ayllu* social structure into a state institution.

LAND DIVISIONS

Land was divided into three parts: to support the gods, to support the emperor and his household and to support the local community. As the emperor was considered divine, the first two categories were both under his control. Their yields supported

priests, shrine attendants and other religious functionaries, and were stored for use in religious ritual and ancestor veneration on appropriate holy days; produce from imperial land was conspicuously stored against future needs in warehouses at provincial capitals.

Left: Terracing and numerous storehouses represent Inca control, and state produce and redistribution – imperial largesse – at the royal estate of Machu Picchu.

Above: The higher one ranked in Inca society the richer one could afford to dress – an Inca elite tunic depicting intricately woven geometric patterns, felines and plants.

Community land was divided into plots and assigned to *ayllus* and households by local *curacas*. Assignment was done annually, so that the proportions allotted could be changed to meet households' changing needs. A similar threefold division was also applied to Altiplano pastureland.

INCA AND PRE-INCA TAXES

The Incas exploited their subjects' sense of reciprocal obligation for state tax purposes. Tax in labour was extracted from both men and women, but labour tax on the two state-owned land divisions applied only to men. This was an annual draft of labour gangs from the *ayllus* and involved work on divine and imperial lands: agriculture and herding, imperial construction projects, military service, transporting goods from state storehouses, or being a runner in the imperial postal service.

We have no pre-Inca records of *mit'a* labour, but archaeologically recognized responses to periodic drought throughout Andean history indicate that *ayllu* and *mit'a* organization was practised and applied across geographical zones. For example, through centuries of lowland drought, *c.*AD1100–1450, the focus of intensive cultivation was gradually shifted from lower, warmer elevations to higher, cooler ones with sufficient rainfall, and to the better-watered eastern Andean slopes. Similarly, on a site scale, the marked adobe bricks of the Huaca del Sol

Below: An imperial Inca accountant with his quipu *record of produce and goods for redistribution, from Poma de Ayala (c.1615).*

pyramid at Middle Horizon Moche show that individual community labour gangs completed different sections.

Another form of state taxation involved textiles. Like reciprocation in textiles within *ayllu* exchange, the value of textiles, calculated in labour, was in effect also a labour tax. Both men and women rendered tribute in cloth production to local governors and to the imperial state. Specified quantities of fibre, wool and cotton were distributed annually, from which men made cordage and rope, and women made cloth. The former was stored and used for all sorts of containers (for example for llama sacks for imperial trade caravans), and for bridge making. Cloth, also stored, was used for the priesthood and the imperial household, as gifts to conquered rulers turned imperial governors, for army kit and for redistribution among communities according to need.

IMPERIAL OBLIGATIONS

Imperial Inca taxation brought vast revenues into state storehouses. The elite proportion of the population that was permanently subsidized by the system was perhaps 10 per cent. There were the higher-ranking decision makers and the lower-ranking implementers of state institutions and projects. The contribution of the first group was, of course, to govern and to preside over religious ritual. They ranged from local to state priests and other religious persons, to local and higher

Above: A symbol of Inca power – a kancha storehouse (reconstructed) at the imperial provincial estate and administrative centre of Ollantaytambo in the Urubamba Valley.

governors and administrators, to conquered royal households, and finally to the imperial household itself.

The second rank comprised individuals who were subsidized because their occupations and technical expertise employed them in non-subsistence jobs. These were the state accountants and historians (the *quipucamayoqs* and *amautas*), agronomists, hydrologists, architects, engineers, surveyors and all the specialist craftspeople employed by the state to produce metalwork, ceramics, masonry, gemstones and woodwork required for the imperial and other ruling households. Some of this production was purely and solely for the cults of the dead.

The distribution of goods from imperial storehouses was not one-directional. The entrenched concept of reciprocity meant that the state also realized and accepted its obligations. The use of state stores was critical to a mutually beneficial relationship between ruler and ruled. Holy days and special days were liberally supplied from the state storehouses with food and drink. Crop failures and other hard times brought by natural disaster could be alleviated through redistribution, according to rank and need, by the state of the goods produced by common labour.

TRADE AND ECONOMY

Neither the Incas nor any pre-Inca culture practised a monetary economy. There was no standard value system with a currency of fixed denominations. There was undoubtedly a sense of value in terms of prized metals, and derived from the efforts to procure commodities, but otherwise value was based on the relative worth of one object or commodity against another, on scarcity, environmental conditions and their effects on annual production, on distance and on the recognized labour involved in production.

ANDEAN VALUES

Even regarding precious metals, it is difficult to understand completely the Inca sense of their value as a contemporary European would have valued them. Metals were mixed, and sometimes the precious metal, say gold, was only a veneer over base metal, making the object appear gold even though it was not pure. This Andean concept of essence – the

Below: These Chimú kero *drinking cups are of gold inlaid with turquoise.*

appearance of an object (what it represented) being more important than the actual substance – is alien to Western ideas of value. Sometimes the precious metal itself was covered in paint.

Moche-Sipán and Lambayeque-Sicán elite burials show that precious objects were lavished on individuals in tombs, showing some sense of the intrinsic worth of precious metal objects on their own merit and as special pieces. Exquisite textiles and ceramics were made by the Nazca and other cultures, not as valued items in this life but as provision, as valued offerings, in the next. Their use was for the deceased in the next phase of their existence. The objects were made specifically for the tomb, and thus not for use until after death. Similarly, the real value of precious metal objects was as offerings to the gods. Their exchange rate was measured in rain to water crops, against a good sea harvest and for protection through appeasement against natural disasters such as earthquakes, flooding or drought, and for the general wellbeing of the people.

Above: Inca state control of textile production and trade can be traced back in Andean history to the earliest times – a Wari tunic of wool and cotton, whose fibres were exchanged between highland and coastal producers.

Textiles were especially valued, and the value of different qualities of textiles was well understood in terms of the labour involved to produce them. In Inca times textiles were the nearest Andean concept to 'coinage', and because their value was understood in terms of labour they were, in effect, reciprocal labour for labour. Because cloth was so highly valued in Andean cultures, it was used by the Incas in a similar way to currency. Regular allocations of cloth were given to army units and it was 'paid' as a reward for government services. Whether textiles were used in this way by any pre-Inca cultures is not known.

STATE-CONTROLLED TRADE

Many commodities were under state control, in terms of control of their production, for example coca growing, or in terms of state redistribution of commodities among the populace. There was also much production under state-commissioned enterprise or industry to provide ceramics, textiles, metal objects and even wooden drinking cups for the extended royal household and government officials and their

households. There were also mass-produced everyday goods, such as eating platters, for feeding *mit'a* labourers.

There was undoubtedly a sense of more highly and less highly regarded objects. No commoner in the Inca Empire used the highly carved and painted *kero* cups that were used by members of the royal household, or wore the sort of precious jewellery worn by elite members of society.

Trade between regions in the Late Horizon was state controlled. How far back into pre-Inca times such state control of trade was practised is hard to ascertain. Yet it seems logical that Inca practices were not late inventions. Rather, the institutionalization of regional trade must have been developed in earlier empires and their societies, such as Tiwanaku and Wari in the Middle Horizon, and by the Early Intermediate Period Moche states and the Kingdom of Chimú in the Late Intermediate Period, in the same area. A major reason for the rise of regional kingdoms was competition for control over resources.

In the Inca state no individual, apart from the emperor, owned land. By imperial decree, all land in the empire

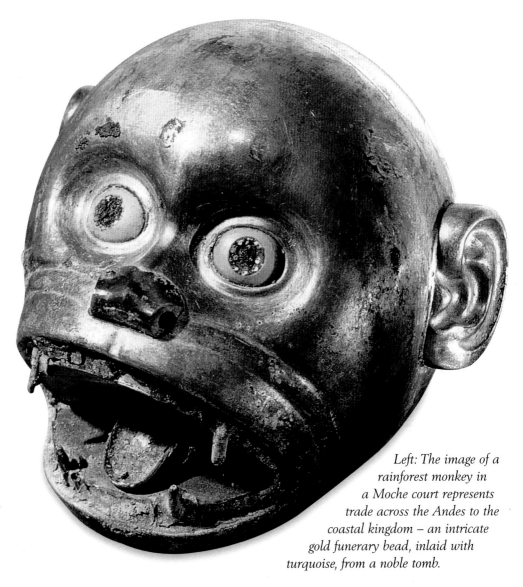

Left: The image of a rainforest monkey in a Moche court represents trade across the Andes to the coastal kingdom – an intricate gold funerary bead, inlaid with turquoise, from a noble tomb.

Below: Transport in ancient Andean cultures was done on the backs of llamas – useless as draught animals, in mountain terrain, carrying side pouches, they were the ideal caravan animals for Andean trade.

belonged to the reigning Sapa Inca. The early development of agriculture throughout the Andean Area shows communal effort for survival.

Irrigation structures had to serve everyone and could not be built piecemeal by individuals. Water, whether it came from rivers whose ultimate source was in the distant mountains or from local rainfall, had to be redistributed from a common source across the landscape to fields, or had to be pooled and moved about among extended terracing and raised fields.

Individuals had rights to work the land but not to sell it. Land was owned by, or its use granted to, the *ayllu* kinship groups.

Individual ownership was limited to personal tools and objects – household tools, ceramics, personal clothing and jewellery – procured through barter or acquired as gifts.

BARTER

Local economies were based on local produce from the communal third land division. Goods were exchanged by barter, redistributed according to need and *ayllu* kinship obligation among households, and exchanged in local markets within and between communities. In bartering between individuals, worth was relative and open to negotiation at the time of exchange.

The ancient use of llama caravans confirms the pre-Inca existence of merchants to move goods between regions. Perhaps the Andean development of such strong *ayllu* kinship reciprocity made the need for a monetary system unnecessary. Where goods from one region to another were available under obligatory exchanges between extended relations, there would have been no need to 'buy' things in the Western sense. Local markets continue to be an endemic part of the Andean economy today.

ANDEAN AND INCA ROADS

Roads and trade routes were part of Andean civilization from early times. The spread of religious ideas and the exchange of highland and lowland commodities obviate the use of established routes. Until the Late Intermediate Period and Late Horizon, however, there is less archaeological evidence.

Water transport was also important. While steep mountain streams were unnavigable, the lower reaches of western coastal rivers were. The sea provided the fastest transport, along the coast between Pacific valleys, and boats criss-crossed Lake Titicaca between cities around its shores. Pizarro's second expedition to South America encountered Inca trading vessels from Tumbes off the north-west coast when he approached the northern border of the empire.

Roads and streets defined city and town plans. Roads from outlying residential areas focused on ceremonial precincts. For example, Nazca settlements were linked by straight routes across intervening desert (for example, from the

Below: The Inca road network was expanded from earlier Middle Horizon roads of the Wari and Tiwanaku empires – spanning seemingly impassable gorges with rope bridges.

ceremonial 'city' of Cahuachi to the 'capital' of Ventilla), and Wari settlements featured regular street grids. Anthony Aveni has described many similarities between the Inca road system and the Nazca lines across long distances.

LIFELINE OF THE EMPIRE

The Inca road system was the lifeline of the empire. Its core was based on earlier established routes. Inca roads connected many former Wari and Tiwanaku Middle Horizon cities and former Wari way stations. The Wari Empire was the first to use its road system for state control. Likewise, the Chimú road system was taken over and improved by the Incas.

Inca roads varied between extremes, from formally constructed, paved roads to narrow paths. John Hyslop has identified and traced more than 23,000km (14,300 miles) of Inca roads, and estimates that the entire Inca system totalled as many as 40,000km (25,000 miles). A main highland route ran along the Andean spine from Cuzco to Quito in northernmost Chinchaysuyu; later, an extension ran into modern Colombia. A second 'trunk' road went south, through north-west Argentina and Chile, from

Above: The Rumicolca route was the entrance to imperial Inca Cuzco, through which royal and noble parties and trader goods entered the city.

Cuzco beyond modern Santiago. Two branches circumnavigated Lake Titicaca and rejoined south of it.

A parallel route ran along the coast, tracing a route from Santiago, across the southern deserts, north-west to the pilgrimage city of Pachacamac, then hugged the mouths of north-west coastal valleys before turning inland to skirt the Sechura Desert. After returning to the coast, it looped back inland to Tumibamba to join the highland route to Quito.

Between trunk routes, roads connected major Inca towns and cities, with as many as 1,000 *tambos* (way stations) along them between cities. Several roads also linked the two major roads at intervals, facilitating highland–lowland trade along ancient routes.

CONSTRUCTION

Difficult terrain was avoided whenever possible. Roads followed the lie of the land, staying below high altitudes by traversing mountain passes and skirting

swamps and deserts. The wheel was unknown in Andean civilization, and the llama is intractable as a draught animal, so apart from litters to carry Inca and other elites, there were no vehicles. Thus road shapes could be adapted to the terrain. Travel was on foot and transport was by load-bearing llama caravans.

Widths of Inca roads varied between *c.*1m and 25m (*c.*3ft and 82ft), sometimes even wider. Mountain roads were narrow, while coastal roads were normally wider and straighter. Although natural contours were followed, the Incas were remarkable for coping when the shorter route was desired or when they encountered what might seem insurmountable obstacles or chasms. Some roads took direct routes, ascending steep slopes, while others used zigzags to lessen the angle of ascent.

Mountain roads often followed cliff faces, and Inca rope suspension bridges spanned deep chasms, anchored at either end with wood or stone superstructures on stone footings. Constant use required frequent repair, yet some Inca bridges were still in use in the 19th century. In a

Below: The Chaka Suyuyuq, *Governor of Bridges, was an important Inca state official, shown here inspecting a rope bridge in Poma de Ayala's* Nueva Corónica, *c.1615.*

few cases, natural stone bridges were used. In other cases, for example at Lake Titicaca, there were reed pontoons across rivers, sections of lake and wet ground, and sometimes travellers were carried across rivers in baskets on cables. There were also river ferries of balsa wood, reed and gourd-float rafts.

Coastal roads were frequently defined by low stone or mud-brick walls, especially to keep desert sands from encroaching, or by rows of wooden posts or stone markers. Side walls lined routes across agricultural lands, and stone pavements formed causeways and canals across wetlands.

TRAVEL

Settlements and *tambos* along the roads served for lodgings and storage. They varied in size according to need, and also often served as seats of local administration. Large *tambos* were located in towns, while smaller ones were sited, theoretically, at intervals of a day's journey apart (in reality they were anywhere from a few hours' walk to a long day's march).

Traders drove llama caravans to transport exotic items between highlands and lowlands and along the coast, but day-to-day necessities were obtained in local barter and by imperial redistribution from provincial stores. General touring was infrequent, except for religious pilgrimage (most likely undertaken by designated representatives, i.e. religious leaders).

Above: The Puyupatamarca way station ruins are one of many along the 'Inca Trail' to Machu Picchu.

Religious processions travelled along the *ceque* system, feeding into the roads to and from the provincial capitals for hostage-holding and sacrificial victims.

IMPERIAL COMMUNICATIONS

Inca roads were a means of control, meant to impress subject peoples with Inca power. They were used to move the army from province to province, to move groups of people (*mitimaes*) among the provinces and for royal pilgrimage. Imperial permission was required to travel on official roads.

Imperial communications between the capital and administrative cities was conducted by a system of runners. Roughly every 1.6km (1 mile) along the major roads, huts were built on either side of the route to shelter a *chasqui* messenger. As a runner approached a hut, he called out and the waiting messenger joined him as he ran. The message was relayed orally and perhaps a *quipu* was passed, after which the fresh messenger ran as fast as possible to the next hut. Messages could be relayed *c.*240km (150 miles) a day in this way; a message could reach Lima on the coast from Cuzco in three days. Each runner served a 15-day rotation and the service was part of the *mit'a* labour obligation.

FARMING, HERDING AND HUNTING

The Andean Area is one of several prime areas in the world where peoples observed and learned to control the cycles of natural plant and animal reproduction, thus domesticating a selection of plants and animals and basing their subsistence on them. Throughout ancient times, subsistence agriculture was supplemented by hunting, fishing and collecting wild animals and plants.

From the Early Horizon the bulk of ancient Andean economy was based on agriculture and llama herding. Hunting, fishing and collecting formed important parts of the economy and were more important in earlier times than later.

Hunting became less important because the staple diet was fixed on the principal food crops, and gradually became the sport of the elite. Fishing on Lake Titicaca remained important for the cultures of the Titicaca Basin and on Lake Poopó to the south. The annual sardine and anchovy runs in the Humboldt Current and the migrations of sea mammals provided important protein sources in the diets of coastal cultures throughout Andean history (and still do).

Below: The other protein and vitamin plant food of ancient Andeans was maize. It was first domesticated in Mesoamerica and its cultivation eventually diffused through to South American ancient cultures.

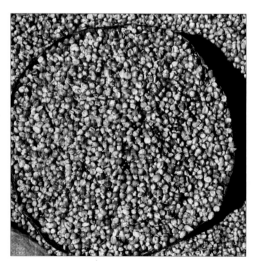

Above: Potatoes were an essential source of carbohydrates and vitamins for Andean peoples, from the collection of wild potato tubers through to their domestication in the Preceramic Period. In winter they were freeze-dried and stored.

Alongside agriculture were the state-organized industries such as textile, ceramic and metal production.

EDIBLE PLANTS

By Inca times a considerable variety of plants and animals was grown, herded and hunted. Principal as a subsistence crop was maize. It was grown both as the staple proportion of dietary intake and for the production of *chicha* beer, used both as a general drink in its weaker form and as an important libation in religious ritual in stronger form.

Other plants were more regional and included potatoes and other tubers (oca and ullucu) in more highland zones, low-altitude tubers such as manioc and yuca, mashwa (a higher-altitude tuber), the high-protein grain quinoa, a variety of beans and also squashes, sweet potatoes, tomatoes, chilli peppers, avocados and peanuts.

Non-edible plants cultivated and/or harvested included coca, cotton, gourds for containers and reeds and fibres for construction and basketry and containers. Tobacco was also grown for medicinal and ritual use. After the earliest phases of domestication, the distribution of these crop plants was primarily altitudinal.

Many plants could be grown in a range roughly from a few metres or yards above sea level to about 1,000m (3,300ft). Others – one variety of chilli pepper, a variety of squash, coca, cotton, gourds, oca, the avocado – were grown in a mid-range zone of about 300–400m (985–1,310ft) above sea level to 1,000–1,500m (3,300–4,920ft). Still others had a much wider range, such as quinoa (28–3,878m/92–12,720ft), the common bean (2–3,700m/6½–12,140ft), potatoes (2–3,830m/6½–12,565ft) and maize (2–3,350m/6½–10,990ft); or a more restricted high-altitude extreme, such as ulluco (an edible tuber, 3,700–3,830m/12,180–12,560ft) and mashwa (850–3,700m /2,788–12,140ft).

Collected plants included wild fruits and many herbs for medicinal and ritual purposes. Eastern forest and tropical hallucinogenic mushrooms were, like

Below: Chilli peppers, first domesticated in the coastal lowlands, added flavour to the staple Andean diet of maize and potatoes.

tropical feathers, traded into the Andean Area. The San Pedro cactus was harvested for its buttons, which are a rich source of hallucinogenic mescaline.

DOMESTICATED ANIMALS

Ancient Andeans domesticated only a few species of animals. The principal herded animals were the llama and the alpaca, both New World camelids. In addition to these, guinea pigs and ducks were bred in captivity or semi-captivity for meat. Dogs were pets and hunting companions, though were also bred for meat.

Herds of llamas and alpacas were kept throughout the highlands, but formed an especially important part of the Altiplano economy of the Titicaca Basin and to the south of it. Here, vast herds were kept and their needs controlled the rhythm of life. The llama and alpaca were kept principally for their wool and as pack animals, but they also provided meat and sacrificial animals, and their bones were used to make into tools.

HUNTING AND FISHING

Hunted land animals were principally deer and the guanaco (the wild camelid from which the llama was domesticated). The fourth New World camelid, the vicuña, was semi-domesticated – herds were trapped, sheared for their extremely soft wool, and released back into the mountains. Wild birds, both coastal and mountain, were also taken, especially eastern tropical rainforest birds for their colourful feathers, although these were mostly bartered for rather than collected directly.

Fishing and shellfish collection supplemented most coastal people's diets, and surpassed agriculture as the main dietary sources in rich coastal areas in earlier periods. Anchovies and sardines were staples in coastal cultures. Sea mammals, especially seals and sea lions, were also hunted. In addition, there were crabs and a wide variety of shellfish. Shellfish were traded to high altitudes in small amounts, and in Inca times fresh seafood was brought to the emperor in a matter of a day or two by *chasqui* runners. Peoples of the Titicaca Basin made extensive use of freshwater fishing.

Left: So important was maize that it was even rendered in silver by imperial craftsmen. It was both secular, as essential food, and sacred, used to make chicha *beer for consumption in religious festivals.*

Above: Maize planting in September, Quya Raymi Killa *or month of the feast of the moon, depicted in Poma de Ayala's* Nueva Corónica, *c.1615.*

COMMUNAL FARMING

In Inca times, agricultural work was separated into repetitive, modular tasks that could be undertaken in succession in the various plots held by individual households. It seems logical to assume that such practices were pre-Inca, although in the various earliest cultures it is uncertain how communal agricultural practices were.

The evidence for communal activities, revealed in monumental architecture, increases at sites in the later Preceramic Period and especially in the Initial Period. It can be argued, therefore, that if labour forces were marshalled for work on building projects, this must have resulted in a division of labour between farmers and builders by which the latter were fed by the former. Alternatively, building projects might have been undertaken during slacker periods of the agricultural year. Even so, communal efforts in architecture may indicate the same for agriculture.

In Preceramic and Initial Period coastal societies, farming in the valleys was separate from the rich fishing and foreshore shellfish collection. However, the two communities obviously needed to cooperate on a communal basis, especially for the cotton fibre that was essential for fishing nets and other tools.

81

irrigation systems. The communal labour foundations of farming, of labour division in societies practising mixed farming and herding economies and of monument building were utilized in building and maintaining canals and required the development of strict rules of access, probably including designated 'officials' to regulate quantities and timing of access to water.

Competition for water and land frequently caused conflict, sometimes leading to open warfare, of which there is ample evidence during some periods of ancient Andean history. Prolonged periods of drought were especially stressful, and caused conflict and population movements.

TERRACING AND RAISED FIELDS

Increasing the amount of land available for crops was achieved in two ways: terracing and raised fields. The steep sides of mountain valleys and the slopes of lower river valleys were modified to create elaborate systems of terracing, often to the point where some terrace 'fields' were only about 1m (3ft) wide. The Inca are famous for their extensive

terracing, which was necessary to feed a growing population and to provide food for the storehouses as insurance against drought years. The co-operative effort required to build and maintain terraces, and to collect and channel rainwater to them, shows high levels of communal organization, which, as with most such practices, were intensified and formalized by the Inca in their *mit'a* labour tax structure.

The same co-operative efforts were required in draining marshlands by digging canals using wooden digging sticks and spades between plots of raised fields – raised with the soil from the channels. Extensive systems of raised-field agriculture surrounded cities in the Titicaca Basin especially. In drought times, when the water level fell, raised fields had to be abandoned, causing population shifts and even the abandonment of cities in the basin.

Ancient Andean fields were fertilized from two principal sources, depending on location: llama dung was the main source of rejuvenating soil nutrients in the sierra and Altiplano, while coastal peoples collected huge amounts of seabird guano from offshore islands to bring to their valley fields. Fish fertilizer was also used by coastal and lake peoples.

Above: Fishing, both in lakes and off the western coast provided essential protein in the Andean diet from the earliest times – Moche pot of a man fishing with a line and bait.

IRRIGATION AGRICULTURE

As populations increased, the richest lands for run-off water agriculture in coastal valleys and rainfall agriculture in the sierra were brought into cultivation. The need for more land surface for growing became acute in coastal plains, mountain valleys and in the Titicaca Basin. To bring water to land farther and farther from rivers, or to channel it from hillsides to mountain valley fields, prompted the invention of

Right: A Moche pot showing two men fishing from a reed raft with a chicha beer jar placed between them.

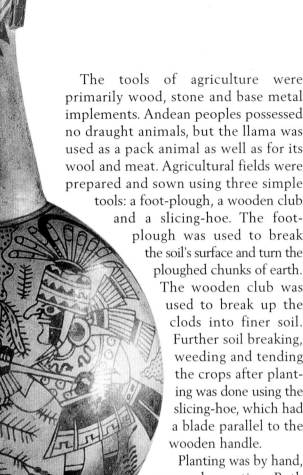

The tools of agriculture were primarily wood, stone and base metal implements. Andean peoples possessed no draught animals, but the llama was used as a pack animal as well as for its wool and meat. Agricultural fields were prepared and sown using three simple tools: a foot-plough, a wooden club and a slicing-hoe. The foot-plough was used to break the soil's surface and turn the ploughed chunks of earth. The wooden club was used to break up the clods into finer soil. Further soil breaking, weeding and tending the crops after planting was done using the slicing-hoe, which had a blade parallel to the wooden handle.

Planting was by hand, as was harvesting. Both men and women worked the fields, especially in non-Inca cultures.

HUNTING AND FISHING

Ancient Andean hunting was done with spears and the *atl-atl* – a stick with a notched end into which the butt of the spear was rested while the other end was held along with the spear shaft. Use of the *atl-atl* greatly extended the distance and power of the weapon when thrown. The bolas (leather strips with stones tied at the ends) was also used; it was thrown so that it wrapped itself around the prey's legs and brought it down for dispatching with spear, club or knife. Birds were also taken with the bolas, and with slings and snares. The bow and arrow was not an Inca weapon, but was used by semi-tropical and tropical peoples.

Fishing was done primarily with nets thrown from small boats, including single-man reed craft on which a fisherman sat astride. Sea mammals were hunted with spears and harpoons 'riding' such craft. Many Moche ceramic pieces depict seal hunts and sea fishing with nets.

Below: The coast at Quebrada la Vaca, near Chala, where the Incas caught fish.

Above: Hunting remained a 'sport', particularly for nobility, through ancient Andean cultures even after it ceased to be a major source of food – Moche ceramic bottle with fine-line depiction of a deer hunt.

INCA FARMING

In Inca agriculture, ploughing, planting and harvesting were done by the assembled workforce plot by plot, but each couple in the force worked designated segments or rows in the plot. This practice of segmentation of labour kept the service rendered and thus the obligational returned service clearly defined. Similarly, if several *ayllu* kinship groups worked on a canal-building project, although each built and maintained a designated section, the entire canal gave benefit to the whole community of fields for which it was built.

CRAFT AND CRAFT WORKERS

Specialized craftsmen and women were among the subsidized people of the Inca Empire. Archaeological evidence that some of the best, finest and most elaborate metalwork, textiles and ceramics were produced especially for burials shows that specialists had been employed by pre-Inca states as well, such as the Moche, Nazca, Wari and Tiwanaku, Lambayeque-Sicán and Chimú. Weaving, ceramic and metalworking compounds have been excavated at sites of these cultures and of the Inca.

Other specialized craftspeople included workers in stone (both masons and gemstone artists), feather workers, and carvers of shell, bone and wood (who made, especially, the decorated *kero* cups for *chicha* beer drinking).

VALUED SPECIALISTS

There was a variety of crafts and a high degree of distinction and expertise within crafts. The fact that craftspeople were

Below: This decorated Moche dish rim depicts a scene of two weavers, possibly a mother teaching her daughter to weave, as well as Moche potters' skill in fine-line decoration.

subsidized highlights their valued places in Inca and pre-Inca societies. Cloth and other crafted goods could be given in exchange within *ayllu* kinship *mit'a* and *ayni* exchange obligations.

WEAVING AND WEAVERS

Weaving was a premier specialized craft from very early times. Textiles preserved in Paracas and Nazca graves reveal the use of intricate patterns, depictions of deities and narrative scenes, and numerous colours, showing the care with which they were made. The numerous layers of mummy bundles demonstrate their importance. Many pieces were included in the mummy wrap before being finished – a clear indication that the pieces were planned specifically for burial and were begun well in advance, most likely when the person was in good health.

Weaving was specifically a female craft, although men worked rougher fibres into cord and rope for more utilitarian uses. In Inca times all women wove, from the common women subjects of the empire, through women of elite households, to the wives of the emperor. For commoners,

Above: From its invention, weaving remained an essential task throughout life – an old woman weaving on a backstrap loom, depicted in Poma de Ayala's Nueva Corónica, *c.1615.*

weaving was a craft and hallmark of femininity in which a woman took pride in clothing her family; to the elite, weaving was a symbolic demonstration of femininity, rather than a necessity. Textile production occupied more people and labour than any other Inca craft, and in intensity of labour was probably surpassed only by agriculture.

CERAMICS AND POTTERS

Pottery, once established and spread among ancient Andean cultures, replaced much of the early roles of rough fibres and gourds for containers, although never completely. Beyond its basic role for practical purposes of storage and cooking (the pots for which were homemade, unspecialized and often plain), ceramics soon became more and more elaborate. Pottery began to serve more than just as containers and took on roles within ritual and burial and as an indication of social rank. Some pots must also have had no purpose other than ornament. At the same time, some pottery simultaneously served, consciously or otherwise, as a record of culture by depicting mythological scenes and scenes of daily life as well as holding liquids and food.

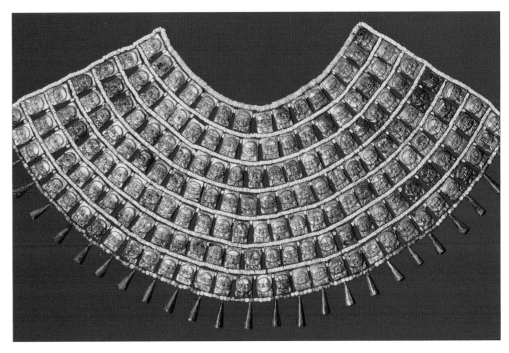

Such increased complexity of design, decoration and use fostered the existence of dedicated potters who could be supplied with food, accommodation and clothing by other members of society. The Incas, and perhaps earlier empires such as Wari and Chimú, established communities of potters specifically to supply uniform vessels. The plates and large, pointed-based, long-necked storage jars used by the Incas in their storehouses to distribute food and drink to *mit'a* workers were uniformly decorated so that there could be no doubt as to the source of the hospitality.

The exquisite craftsmanship of Moche pottery has always stood out among Andean wares. Not only are Moche ceramics a source of narrative information through scene painting on red-on-cream vessels, but also many Moche ceramic

Below: Finely woven Paracas wool textiles in southern coastal Peru reveal trade for Altiplano wool and depict ritual decapitation for the cult of trophy heads. Their complexity and use as mummy wraps involved their preparation through one's lifetime.

pieces are clearly portraiture and depictions of specific rituals, including shamanism, animalistic transformation, healing, combat and sexual acts.

METALLURGY AND METALLURGISTS

A third premier craft in ancient Andean society was metalworking. Exquisite, elite gold, silver, copper and alloy pieces were made from Paracas and Nazca times. Metalworkers flourished in Moche culture and later in the Lambayeque-Sicán and Chimú states – all three successive cultures in the north-west coastal valleys.

Above: A silver pectoral from a Late Intermediate Period rich lord's tomb in the Lambayeque Valley is one of thousands of examples of the superb minute craftsmanship of ancient Andean metalsmiths.

This is perhaps not surprising, as they are geographically the closest to the areas in modern-day Colombia and Ecuador where the earliest, and most elaborate, metallurgy in the Americas developed.

Gold and silver were used extensively, both by the Incas and pre-Inca peoples. These metals were used exclusively for luxury jewellery and ritual objects. They were used both pure and as gilding and plate, and in some cases were even covered with paint. Many specialist pieces, for example gold and silver llama figurines, were made especially for burial with a sacrificial victim. Among the Incas, gold and silver were restricted to use by the nobility. Commoners could use only copper or bronze (a copper and tin, or arsenic, alloy), but the craftsmanship involved in the manufacture of such base-metal objects was no less skilled.

Copper was made into items of personal adornment, such as pins to fasten clothing, pendants, earrings, bracelets and armlets; also for sheet-copper burial masks and for *tumi*, crescent-shaped sacrificial knives. Copper is too soft for tools, so in addition to jewellery, bronze was used to make axes, knives, chisels, pins and tweezers, and the heads for war clubs.

MILITARY SERVICE AND WARFARE

We know little of the pre-Inca armies, except that they were successful in conquering and controlling large areas. The Moche were particularly warlike; the Naymlap legend may be an Early Intermediate folk memory of the invasion of the Lambayeque Valley, establishing the late Moche dynasty by conquest.

EARLY CONFLICT

Early warfare is depicted in stone and ceramics. The more than 300 carved slabs at Initial Period Cerro Sechín have been interpreted as a war memorial. The large slabs, which constitute about 7 per cent of the total slabs, portray a procession of triumphant warriors wearing pillbox hats and loincloths, and carrying staffs and darts. Other slabs show the disembodied remains of the vanquished, and at least one warrior has a decapitated head dangling from his waist. Two slabs carved with banners flank the compound's central gateway.

Are these sculptures evidence of small-scale, seasonal raiding between towns? Or are they commemorating a great historical victory, or a symbolic battle, rather than a specific event? Another view argues that the scene is an elaborate hallucinogenic ritual. One slab depicts toad eggs (representing toads known to carry hallucinogens?). Disembodiment is typical of Andean hallucinogenic transformation.

Cerro Sechín dates to the beginnings of Andean civilized society, when towns were becoming cities, and their locations and spacing across the landscape imply conflict and equidistant positioning in competition for resources, especially water. Early Intermediate Period Nazca pots show battle scenes – complex depictions of intertwined warriors in chaotic mêlées.

RITUAL COMBAT

Moche battle scenes usually depict pairs of warriors, both Moche. They are thought to depict ritual combat rather than scenes of conquest. The Huaca de la Luna walls at Moche, however, and at Huaca Cao Viejo near by, are painted with ranks of armed warriors, leaving little

Above: As well as building an empire through conquest, the Moche had a cult of celebrated 'gladiatorial' or ritual combat, as depicted here on a moulded spouted bottle.

doubt that Moche Sipán Lords, buried with war clubs and other war regalia, were military leaders as well as statesmen. Accompanying tombs include warrior burials, and Moche metalwork frequently depicts individual warriors.

Moche city-states saw frequent conflict. Individual combat scenes may represent minimal battles between rival Moche city-states, much as Black Figure paintings did in ancient Greece. This interpretation is in keeping with the ancient Andean concept of 'essence'.

Left: One of the best-known portrayals of ancient Andean warfare is the Cerro Sechín highland temple of sculpted slabs that forms the wall around the temple complex, including both victorious warriors and the severed heads of the defeated.

The Middle Horizon Tiwanaku and Wari empires were built by conquest. Each expanded within its territory, and maintained frontiers with fortresses. Wari expansion was marked by stone forts with regimented barrack-like planning – for example at Cerro Baúl in the Moquegua Valley and Pikillacta, strategically located in the Cuzco Valley roughly halfway between the two imperial capitals of Huari and Tiwanaku.

ARMS, ARMOUR, TACTICS

Andean warfare was conducted in pitched battles of hand-to-hand fighting, until one side broke. A pair of hammered gold and silver Wari figures portrays imposing warriors holding shields and spear-throwers, wearing four-cornered helmets and geometrically patterned rectangular tunics. Their whole composition

Left: A spouted, polished, moulded effigy bottle of a warrior with his spear and feathered war bonnet – Moche, showing earlier Chavín-style influence.

resembles the rectangular, compartment-like nature of Wari military architecture and is not dissimilar to Inca soldiers in their chequered tunics. A Wari vessel depicts heavily armed warriors kneeling in a flotilla of reed boats, apparently on a raid heading towards Tiwanaku across Lake Titicaca.

Late Intermediate and Late Horizon conflict is demonstrated in Inca legendary history. Typical is the tale of the turning point in Inca history – the defeat of the Chanca and the establishment of Pachacuti's reign. The provincial garrisoned town of Huánuca Pampa near Quito includes both identifiable barracks in the north of the city and 700 storage houses for tribute, army rations and civilian stores.

Weapons were similar to those for hunting: clubs, knives, spears and spear-throwers, slings and the bolas. The bow and arrow was known, but was not an Andean weapon – the Incas employed bowmen from the rainforest. The bolas was thrown at an enemy's legs to bring him down, after which he could be speared or clubbed to death. Warriors carried shields (Inca shields were rectangular or trapezoidal) and wore quilted cotton armour. Inca soldiers depicted in Guaman Poma de Ayala's *Nueva Corónica y Buen Gobierno, c.1615*, wear black-and-white chequered tunic uniforms and are shown in ranked squadrons in battle and storming city walls.

INCA CONQUEST

The success of Inca imperial expansion is undoubtedly the result of superior military leadership and organization. As territories were conquered and assimilated into Inca society, the army increasingly comprised recruits

Above: An Inca warrior presenting a severed head, from Poma de Ayala's Nueva Corónica, *c.1615.*

from conquered peoples. Service in the army was part of the *mita'a* labour tax. Another factor in Inca military success was their catering organization: Inca roads and storehouses for military supplies made deployment in far-flung provinces rapid and efficient.

Some provinces were subdued without battle, the people being persuaded that submission to the Incas was preferable to resistance. Confrontation always ended in defeat, immediately or eventually. Battle against an Inca army resulted in many killed. Inca terms of conquest, either after submission or defeat, were the same – 'fair' but severe. If a city or people submitted without a fight, no one was killed. All land was transferred to state ownership and the Incas gave the conquered people permission to use it. Produce was divided into three parts: for the state (meaning the royal household), for the state religion and for the people. Local leaders were usually retained and incorporated into Inca state structure. Sons of local leaders were taken to Cuzco to be trained in Inca statecraft and policy, and were then made leaders when their fathers died. Similarly, local shrines were left, but idols were often removed to Cuzco as hostages, and could be damaged or destroyed as punishment for rebellion.

CIVIL SERVANTS AND JUSTICE

The division between a royal or imperial household and members of a state civil service is not an easy one. The entourage of the legendary King Naymlap included a number of special court posts whose holders accompanied the king and performed specific duties exclusively for him.

CIVIL SERVICES

Without records, we have no knowledge of pre-Inca civil duties, but can surmise that there must have been some informal or formal organization for urban planning and maintenance. An annual round of religious ceremony must have been in the hands of the priests. Daily secular administration must have been in the hands of citizens appointed by rulers or chosen by the mutual agreement of some members of society (e.g. the 'elders'). As always, these functions in pre-Inca society were obviously fulfilled but until the Incas we have little evidence of how they were organized or performed.

The Incas copied much from those who came before them, as a continuum in Andean civlization's evolution. We can therefore only assume that what little we know of civil administration from the Inca records might also apply in pre-Inca

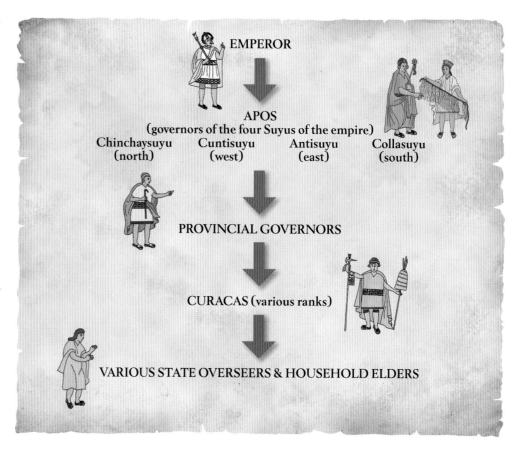

Above: Diagram of the Inca imperial government administrative hierarchy, showing delegation of power from the Sapa Inca *through* apo suyu *and provincial governors, curacas and household elders.*

urban society, such as the kingdoms of the Chimú and the Moche, or the empires of the Wari and Tiwanaku.

Many workers in the Inca state economy and social organization, who would be called civil servants in modern Western society, were either appointees of the emperor or draftees of the *mit'a* labour system such as record-keepers, storehouse administrators, road engineers or messenger runners.

GOVERNMENT APPOINTEES

Government posts comprised appointed individuals in a hierarchy based on heredity and/or ability. The highest ranks, the *apo* appointees of the emperor, governed each of the four *suyu* divisions of the empire. Those below them were also

Left: An imperial Inca prison with prisoner depicted in Poma de Ayala's Nueva Corónica, *c.1615.*

appointees, as governors of provinces and *curacas* of decreasing numbers of households. The day-to-day regulation of labour was in the hands of household elders.

Other administrative roles included the court historians and record-keepers, overseers in state workshops for the production of pottery, metalwork and textiles, clerks to oversee the collection and redistribution of goods in the state storehouses, and engineers and military commanders. Owners of imperial and noble estates chose their own administrators, which were thus private appointments, but the functions they performed were similar to those of civil servants on state lands.

Amautas (historians) and *quipucamayoqs* (record-keepers) were selected from the nobility and their posts became hereditary; army commanders likewise. There was formal training for these jobs. Other civil servants were no doubt selected for their skills and aptitudes for the tasks, having been trained on the job. Many were no doubt also hereditary in practice.

RULES

Performing these jobs in Inca society was according to established 'rules', allegedly established by the ninth emperor, Pachacuti, who also decreed the punishments applicable to each type of crime. There were quotas of agricultural produce, numbers of pots, tools, weapons and jewellery, lengths of cloth, and sections of road, irrigation canals, terracing or buildings set by imperial decree to be fulfilled.

Below: Vilcashuamán was an Inca administrative centre with a large plaza flanked by the Temple of the Sun and with an ushnu *platform.*

Successful fulfilment of quotas, keeping the peace, and efficiency in administering the *mit'a* labour tax was rewarded. Failure was treated by a regime increasing punishment from public humiliation to beatings to execution. There were also prisons for holding suspects and criminals.

ADMINISTRATION OF JUSTICE

Application of Inca law was part of the administrative system and presided over by the *curacas* (officials below Inca provincial governors, in charge of a certain number of households) of the places in which the crimes were committed. Cases involving parties within the same division of 100 households, for example, were ruled on by the appropriate *curaca* of those 100 households; a case that involved individuals from different units of 100 households was presided over by the *curaca* of the 500 households in which the two smaller divisions resided. Trials were normally within five days of being caught; punishment was immediate upon conviction.

Above: Capital punishment by stoning was the ultimate fate of convicted adulterers in Inca society, here depicted in Poma de Ayala's Nueva Corónica, *c.1615.*

Inca *curacas* were given rewards for doing a good job, but if the opposite were the case, they too were punished. Punishment for laziness might be a public and humiliating rebuke by the provincial governor. Gross misconduct and dishonesty, such as abusing the *mit'a* system or embezzling state property, was punishable by execution.

Punishments for violating the laws were strict and could be severe. They included capital punishment. When the crime was one punishable by death, the case was overseen by the provincial governor rather than by a *curaca*. For if a *curaca* executed a person without the permission of his governor, he would have a heavy stone dropped on his back from a height of about 1m (3ft); if he committed the transgression a second time, he was put to death.

There were no formal courthouses as such, although the open, high-walled courtyards called *kanchas* must have included buildings among those surrounding their plazas specifically for hearing criminal cases. The *ushnu* platforms in such courtyards might have been used for this purpose.

The Spanish Colonial administration naturally placed Spaniards in the highest ranks of their new government. But at more local levels, like the Incas before them, they continued to use native leaders.

PRIESTS AND SHAMANS

Throughout Andean civilization, priests existed, residing at temples and pilgrimage sites. The oracle above the Lanzón monolith in the Old Temple at Early Horizon Chavín de Huántar must have had priests to act in giving answers to supplicants. Later, the oracle at Pachacamac had similar specialists. From the Initial Period, temple buildings and precincts must have served as places to instruct acolytes into the priesthood by in-service training.

The rich Early Intermediate Period Moche burials, and those of the Late Intermediate Period Sicán-Lambayeque,

Below: A Moche pottery jar representing a shaman holding a wooden stick used to prepare coca balls.

appear to be of priests or lords. Moche ceramics and murals depict several scenes of priests and priestesses administering at ritual ceremonies.

GODS OR PRIESTS?

It is often difficult to tell, however, if the stone sculpture and other depictions in many Andean cultures are of priests or of the gods themselves. For example, the Early Horizon Pukará Decapitator figure depicts a seated male figure, holding an axe and a severed head. His cap is decorated with supernatural faces. He is either a supernatural composite being, or a man wearing a representative mask with a fanged mouth. Similarly, buried at the base of the western staircase of the Akapana temple at Middle Horizon Tiwanaku was a black basalt image of a seated, puma-headed person (a *chachapuma*), also holding a severed head. Another Tiwanaku *chachapuma* sculpture is of a standing figure holding a severed head. Are these representations of the gods or of priests impersonating them?

In early civilizations it seems likely that rulers and priests were the same, or were of the same family. Separate roles were evident in some cultures, however, as shown in the story of Fempellec. This twelfth ruler of the Naymlap Dynasty, sometime in the late Middle Horizon or early Late Intermediate Period, came into conflict with the priests of Chot when he attempted to remove the idol of Yampallec to another city. The story also demonstrates the considerable power of priests in at least this Andean society, for the priests, acting for the gods and in behalf of the people, expelled Fempellec.

RELIGIOUS POWER

The power of religious cults, and thus the influence of priests, is amply shown by the Early Horizon spread of the Chavín Cult. Earlier, the Kotosh Tradition may have been the earliest such regional Andean cult. The cult and priests of

Above: A terracotta model of a shaman with an elaborate headdress from the Jamacoaque culture, Ecuador.

Pachacamac, an oracle and pilgrimage centre that endured more than a millennium on the central Peruvian coast, certainly exercised great power, for they were even recognized and honoured by the Inca emperors. Such was the power of the cult that priests of distant communities solicited the Pachacamac priests for permission to establish branch shrines in their home towns to the creator god Pachacamac. If deemed to have the ability to support cult activities, a priest from Pachacamac was assigned to the new shrine and the community supplied labour and produce from assigned lands to support him and the shrine. Part of the produce was kept for the shrine and

Above: This elaborate hand-painted French wallpaper dates from 1826 and shows the European fascination with Inca sun worship.

the rest sent back to Pachacamac. Such branches were thought of as the wives, children or brothers and sisters of the main cult city.

SHAMANS AND HEALERS

Temple priests were supplemented in local communities by shamans and healers. The careful preparation and mummification of bodies before burial at Chinchorros as early as 5000 BC, and at the Paracas and Nazca cemeteries demonstrate their early existence. Many Moche pots portray men and women healers at work, laying on hands and administering herbs and drugs.

Transformation, in which a priest or shaman changed into another being (part-human, part-beast), is a common Andean religious theme. From the Initial Period onwards, wall sculptures, murals and depictions on pottery and textiles show figures in various states of transformation. Some of the earliest are the Initial Period wall paintings of insects with human heads at Garagay, the wall sculptures of shamanic trance at Moxeke and the staged stone sculpture of jaguar transformation in the Early Horizon sunken circular court at Chavín de Huántar. Spiders with human heads were frequently depicted in the Moche and later cultures.

Drug paraphernalia has frequently been found among grave goods, but a unique late 5th-century AD cave burial near Wari is that of a local medicine man, herbalist or shaman. He was accompanied by his tools: a wooden snuff tablet decorated with a Tiwanaku 'attendant angel' figure, a basket with multicoloured, front-facing deity figures and various herbal plants.

PRIESTS AND PRIESTESSES

Inca priests and priestesses were full-time specialists, supported by the state. A third of conquered lands were designated for their upkeep. Such a large portion indicates that there was a correspondent sector in Inca society devoted to state religion.

Inca priests were organized into a hierarchy resembling that of the Inca civil service. Priestly ranking went according to the importance, and thus rank, of the shrine he served. The top priest was a close relative of the emperor, and the high priest of the state cult of Inti (the sun). Each of the chief priests or priestesses of the other five principal Inca deities came next in rank, each housed in a separate *wasi* (chamber) in the Coricancha: Viracocha (creator), Quilla (Moon), Chaska-Qoylor (Venus), Illapa (thunder, lightning) and Cuichu (rainbow). A similar hierarchy existed in each shrine or temple, from the chief shrine priest or priestess down to his or her attendants and trainees.

Left: A lively terracotta figurine of a shaman wearing a headdress decorated with snake heads and dancing during a ceremony of the Bahía culture, Manabí, Ecuador.

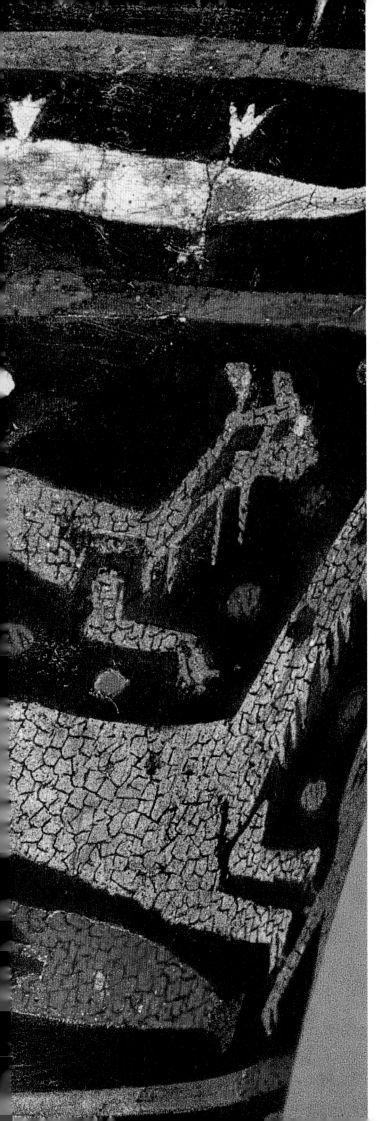

CHAPTER FIVE

DAILY LIFE

Most of what we know about the daily lives of ordinary people in Inca and pre-Inca times comes from archaeological evidence. The private lives and education of Inca subjects is hardly commented on in the early Spanish sources, whose authors were more interested in the lives of the Inca emperors and in the workings of the *mit'a* labour tax system and collection of wealth. Native writers, such as Garcilasco de la Vega and Felipe Guaman Poma de Ayala, give some information on daily life, and the 398 drawings in the latter's book show many aspects of Inca life and culture.

Archaeological work has concentrated on the more monumental and central areas of sites, or on wide aerial studies of sites in their settings. Much work also focuses on the art of Andean civilization and on the most spectacular objects. As a result, we know less about the ordinary ancient Andean. We know little of the daily routines followed by most subjects of the empire, except that they must have been taken up by a regular annual cycle required by an agricultural way of life for most people.

For the ordinary citizen, life in Inca times would have been a repetitive round of routine tasks and mutual obligations within one's *ayllu* kinship group, punctuated or relieved by *mit'a* labour tax duties for the state, and by a regular schedule of religious ceremony and festivity. In earlier times, as civilized state societies increased in territorial control, population and administrative complexity, divisions within societies of different tasks created more varied roles for different groups of citizens.

Left: Inca kero *cup showing a man hunting llamas with* bolas, *a weapon using cords weighted at the ends.*

COMMUNITY, HOUSEHOLD AND ADULTHOOD

Andean society was based around the family household, and family structure and ritual bound society together.

COMMUNITY

From the early farming villages of the Initial Period and Early Horizon, much larger towns, and eventually cities, developed near or around increasingly large and elaborate ritual centres. The building of such sites required some form of civil control and organization of labour on a formal basis, most likely utilizing the forms of kinship obligations that developed in agricultural communities.

Andean cultures did not formally divide state and religion, although as civilization developed there were specialist leaders, rulers, administrators and priests. In everyday life, civil duties and religion appear always to have been mixed in the daily tasks of making a living, seasonal work routines and an annual cycle of ritual and supplication to the gods for prosperity and wellbeing.

Nevertheless, certain sites were devoted to religious and ritual activities, while other sites were the thriving towns and cities of residents engaged in

Below: Silver Inca figurines of an alpaca, whose long, fine wool was used in the finest textiles, a llama and a female votive figure.

day-to-day agricultural tasks, community and state administration and regulation of the economy.

HOUSEHOLD

The household was the basic unit of most Andean societies. Agricultural families were nuclear, but indications are that the formal kinship ties (*ayllu*) described in the sources for the Incas and their subjects in the Late Horizon were developments from much earlier times. Their formulation and development probably began and operated on some scale to regulate labour and economy from the beginnings of village and town life. In Inca society, both men and women lived in their parent's household until marriage.

Daily tasks were planting, tending and harvesting crops, herding llamas, hunting and fishing, making household items, building and repairing houses, irrigation structures and terracing, and making cloth, clothing, jewellery, and weapons and tools.

While men worked in the fields or were away on

Above: Originally spreading to South America from Mesoamerica via the Central American cultures, maize remained a daily staple of the Andean diet.

mit'a labour service for the emperor, the daily domestic chores of cooking, cleaning and washing were done by women. Before the Inca conquest, gender roles were less differentiated: women helped in agriculture, men span, wove and made pottery as well as women.

As inheritance in Inca society was through both the father's and mother's sides of the family, a noblewoman could own land and llama herds in her own right. Women thus controlled a certain proportion of Inca economic resources, but it is unknown how much.

PUBERTY AND ADULTHOOD

A girl's puberty began with her first menstruation, shortly after which a ceremony was held to recognize this life transition. The girl remained in the house for three days, during which she could eat nothing until the third day, when she was allowed some raw maize. On the fourth day, her mother bathed her and plaited her hair. Relatives assembled at the house. The girl dressed in new clothes made for the occasion, came out

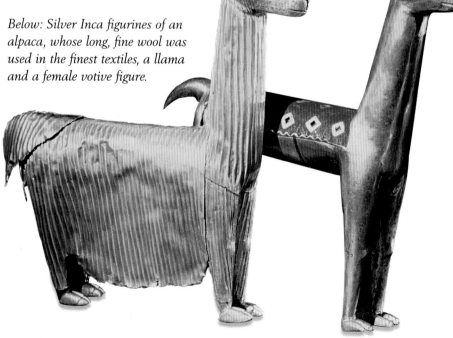

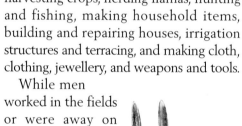

of confinement and served food and drink to the assembly. Her most important uncle pronounced her permanent name and, as at the first-naming ceremony, she received gifts.

Inca boys' puberty was marked by a common ritual, held at age 14 (considered to coincide roughly with the onset of puberty). For commoners, the ceremonies were less elaborate than they were for boys from the Inca royal, noble and elite provincial classes. The principal purpose was to initiate boys as men and warriors, and as proper members of Inca society. The rituals took place over three weeks, requiring preparation during the preceding several months. Mothers made their sons fine garments specifically for the ceremonies.

Below: The popularity of 're-recreating' Inca ceremony and ritual incorporates modern elements (laced shoes and balloons) as well as 'traditional' textiles.

In November, the boys went on pilgrimage to the Inca sacred mountain of Huanacauri, near Cuzco (or a local sacred mountain in the province). Each boy led a llama. He asked the spirit of the mountain for permission to perform the ceremonies of puberty. The llamas were sacrificed by having their throats slit and a priest smeared the blood across each boy's face. Each boy received a sling to signify his warrior status. The boys danced, then performed certain ritual 'chores': collecting

Above: A typical Inca house was open plan with a central hearth and a trapezoidal doorway. Most household activities were performed outdoors.

straw for their relatives to sit on at the final ceremony and chewing maize to ferment *chicha* beer for the ceremonies.

The formal puberty rites took place in December, within the Capac Raymi summer solstice festival. The initiates made a second pilgrimage to Huanacauri, where they sacrificed more llamas. When they returned home, waiting relatives whipped them on their legs to make them strong and brave. The boys performed a sacred dance and drank *chicha*.

After a week's rest, they sacrificed more llamas, were whipped again, and performed a dance atop the hill of Anahuarque near Huanacauri (or other local sacred *huaca*). The boys then raced down the hill's rugged terrain; at the bottom, girls from the same class gave them more *chicha*.

The next task was to walk to several other hills around Cuzco, then receive a loincloth in formal recognition of manhood. The final visit was to the sacred spring of Callispuquio, where initiates were met by relatives who gave them their warrior's weapons: a boy's principal uncle gave him a shield, sling and war mace; other relatives lectured him on the proper male and Inca noble conduct. His ears were pierced for earplugs that marked his status as an Inca noble (or provincial elite) and warrior.

FOOD AND DRINK

The wide variety of early domesticated plants exploited by ancient Andeans provided the basic diet, which was supplemented by hunting and fishing, depending on local availability. Sea fishing and shellfish, for example, were more important at coastal sites, as was fishing at Lake Titicaca and other Altiplano lakes. In the sierra, hunting was mostly for a small number of mammals and rodents after the large game animals of the late Ice Age had become extinct.

FROM HUNTER-GATHERING TO GROWING

In the Archaic Period, hunting and gathering prevailed and at rock shelters and cave sites such as Pachamachay and Guitarrero almost all faunal and floral remains are of wild varieties hunted and collected. Even in the Preceramic Period the wild components of bone and plant remains at sites such as Kotosh, La Galgada, Huaricoto, Salinas de Chao and

Below: The elaborate channelling and distribution of water was essential for Andean daily household use as well as for agriculture. Fountains at Inca Yupanqui's imperial lodge at Tambo Machay.

others, including caves still occupied in the Ayacucho and Calejón de Huaylas, are high.

Coastal sites were able to rely on hunting and collecting of shellfish well into the late Preceramic Period because the coastal food sources were so abundant. Only from the Initial Period onwards, when the domestic flora and fauna remains at sites predominate, can we see the full range of domesticated plants and animals from the physical changes brought through domestication.

DAILY DIET

We cannot know the daily meal routines of pre-Inca cultures. It may or may not be legitimate to project what we know from Inca records back into pre-Inca times.

The principal foods of Andean peoples were maize, potatoes, oca and ulluca (both tubers), quinoa and tarwi (high-protein grains), and kidney, lima and string beans and squashes. More regional staples included peanuts, manioc and mashwa (a higher-altitude tuber). These were supplemented with a variety of herbs as seasoning, especially chilli peppers and mint, and with fruits and nuts (both

Above: An elaborately decorated Inca kero *cup depicts a puma or jaguar, an ever-present religious image woven into daily use.*

domesticated and wild), including peanuts and cashews, tomatoes, pumpkins, palmettos, pineapples, sour cherries, custard apples, cactus fruits, elderberries, guavas, avocados and an ancient variety of banana. Animal protein, including fish, was available, but the main sources of meat in the highlands were guinea pigs and ducks. Llama and deer meat was also eaten.

Locally, day-to-day meals were fairly staple and monotonous, though redistribution of foodstuffs between highlands and lowlands made it less so. Local markets supplied by traders provided the opportunity to barter for highland and lowland produce. Nevertheless, commerce in the Inca Empire was virtually non-existent because all aspects of the economy were so regulated by the state. Within provinces, people were allowed to have local markets, where they could exchange everyday foods and other items such as tools and common jewellery. Luxury

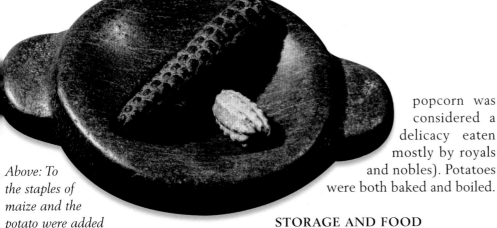

Above: To the staples of maize and the potato were added numerous gourds and herbal condiments ground in wooden mortars.

items and exotic foods, however, were held in the state's monopoly and were produced, collected and stored by the state.

Apart from water, the main drink was *chicha* – weakly fermented beer made from maize and several other plants. Although it was drunk daily, it also played a significant role in religious ritual and in life-stage ceremonies. Bernabé Cobo claims that water was only drunk when no *chicha* was available!

COOKING AND EATING

The Incas ate only two meals a day: a morning meal (8–9 o'clock) and early evening meal (4–5 o'clock). Meals were taken seated on the ground outdoors, with the women facing the cooking pots and sitting back-to-back with the men.

It is not known whether different foods or combinations of foods were consumed for the different meals. Ordinary people ate off flat pottery plates and drank from wooden or ceramic beakers (*kero* cups). Royals and nobles ate and drank from copper, gold and silver plates and cups.

Cooking was done in ceramic pots set on tripods or pedestals placed directly over the fire. Food was both boiled and roasted in the flames. Mixed foods in soups and stews were common as the main dishes. Maize was prepared in several ways, including roasting on the cob, in stews, as a kind of baked or boiled cornbread, and popped (although

popcorn was considered a delicacy eaten mostly by royals and nobles). Potatoes were both baked and boiled.

STORAGE AND FOOD PROCESSING

Foodstuffs and *chicha* were stored in the house in large ceramic jars, usually with pointed bases to stabilize them in the ground. Uncooked household storage was kept in attics and rafter space, or in mud-plastered cornstalk bins, or in mud-lined floor-pits. General harvest and main stores were kept in outdoor adobe brick buildings until needed in the house. Maize, peanuts and other grains and nuts were stored dry.

Right: Inca ceramic figurine of a parrot eating a rather plump maize cob or gourd links western coastal food with a tropical import.

Meat, fish and potatoes were freeze-dried for preservation and storage. Freeze-drying was done in the cold, dry winter. Meat (*charqui*) and fish were cut into thin strips, pounded, then left to dry in the sun during the day and freeze at night. Potatoes were soaked in water to soften them, then left to freeze at night; during the day, thawing evaporated the water. Repeated freezing and thawing eventually left the dried pulp (*chuño*). Freeze-drying enabled the Incas to store large quantities of staples in state storehouses (*collcas*) for imperial use and for redistribution, and made food much easier to transport.

Chicha was made by chewing the maize kernels (or other seeds) to split the pulp, then spitting the mash into jars of warm water. Salivary enzymes broke down the sugars in the pulp and began fermentation. For daily *chicha*, fermentation was allowed for a few days. Longer fermentation produced stronger *chicha* for religious use.

BIRTH, CHILDHOOD AND EDUCATION

Birth in Inca society, like all events through life, was considered part of a great cycle. Death was not an end, rather the continuation of the cycle in a different state of being. Other significant Inca childhood events were the first haircut and recognition of the onset of puberty; later rituals were marriage, then death and burial.

BIRTH

There were no special places for birth to take place, and it was not an especially marked event. Women relatives might assist at the time of birth, in the house. A woman simply delivered the child, then took it to the nearest stream to bathe herself and the baby. The newborn child was carried in a cloth sling for the first four days of its life and was then laid in a cradle. It then spent most of its life in either a sling or a cradle until it could walk. Garcilasco de la Vega

Below: As most daily activities took place outdoors, Inca babies were kept warm and close-by swaddled in layers of textiles (month-old baby from Poma de Ayala's Nueva Corónica, c.1615).

claims that Inca women never picked up their babies to suckle or play with them, lest they became 'cry babies', but it can hardly be the case that women did not regularly suckle their babies until they could take solid food.

More or less immediately after birth, a woman returned to her daily duties in the household. It is likely that elite women had an easier experience, and there were *yanaconas* (servants or personal attendants) to help at birth and in nursing and raising the child.

CHILD-NAMING

In Inca society, the naming of a child was delayed until it was weaned, at about 1 year old. This was known as the 'first-naming' and was associated with the child's first haircut. To mark the event, the parents gave a party to honour the child, to which they invited relatives and friends. The party included much drinking, music-making and dancing, and must have provided welcome relief from daily routines. The party came to an end when the eldest male relative cut a piece of the child's hair and trimmed his/her nails. Then he gave the chosen name. Other relatives cut locks of the child's hair and presented gifts to it.

The name given at this ceremony was used throughout childhood, but was not considered permanent, for a lifelong name was not given until the child reached maturity, marked by puberty ceremonies. The onset of puberty was considered the

Left: Moche potters depicted every scene imaginable, including this scene of a woman giving birth, helped by two 'midwives', on a stirrup-spout bottle.

end of childhood and beginning of adulthood, and the event was marked by special, different, initiation rituals for boys and girls.

PLAY

There is little evidence of toys, but play must have been part of a child's life, perhaps learning to play a flute or drum, making miniature pots and clothing for figurines, and dancing.

Much of childhood was occupied in learning household activities appropriate and achievable as the child grew up. When strong enough, boys began to help with farming tasks and with herding animals. They also began to learn skills with weapons, both for hunting and for eventually serving in the army, and perhaps accompanied adult men when they went hunting and fishing. Girls helped with the numerous household

Above: Andean boys and girls took on daily chores and daily responsibilities at an early age. This Inca boy depicted in Poma de Ayala's Nueva Corónica, c.1615, *hones his hunting and warrior skills with a sling.*

chores of preparing meals, cleaning, spinning and weaving, and minding younger sisters and brothers.

EDUCATION

There was no formal state education in Inca society, or, as far as we know, in any pre-Inca culture, at least not for all boys and girls. No archaeological evidence can be clearly identified as a place of learning or instruction, although from the Initial Period onwards temple buildings and precincts must have served as places to instruct acolytes into the priesthood by in-service training.

Likewise, the skills needed for farming, fishing, hunting, spinning, weaving, potting, metalworking, construction and any other daily tasks and crafts were basically taught in the home by parents or by practising professionals to novices in workshops or on-site in informal apprenticeships. With no writing system in any Andean civilization, all knowledge was obviously passed on verbally and by demonstration.

There are only four exceptions to this picture. The first two are the Inca state accountants and historians (*quipucamay-oqs* and *amautas*), whose positions were nevertheless hereditary and therefore taught to sons by their fathers. The only

boys and girls who were taught in a 'school' were the sons of Inca and provincial nobles, and the girls chosen to become *acllas* (or *acllyaconas*), 'chosen women' to serve in the state cult of Inti (the sun), and some as imperial concubines or to become 'gifts' in imperial political alliances.

The sons of the nobility (including provincial *curacas*) received four years of education at a school in Cuzco. Their teachers were the *amautas*, who taught them Quechua (the Inca language) in the first year, Inca religion in the second, *quipu* 'reading' in the third and Inca history in the fourth. Learning was by rote through memorization and repetition, and through practice. Discipline was strict and included beatings, although these were restricted to a single beating per day – striking the soles of the feet 10 times with a cane. The principal purpose of this education of the sons of nobles and provincial *curacas* was to indoctrinate them as loyal subjects for when they took up leadership in local administration.

Girls were chosen to become *acllyaconas* at about 10; they were selected from the daughters of conquered peoples. They were first taken to a provincial capital, where they were taught in the *acllahuasi* (house of the *acllya-conas*) cloisters for four years: learning to spin, weave, cook, make *chicha* (beer), and the elements of Inca religion, especially how to serve Inti (the sun). Then they were taken to Cuzco and presented to the emperor, who decided whether they were to enter the Cuzco *acllahuasi*, become

part of the emperor's court (perhaps one of his concubines) or be given in marriage or concubinage to a provincial governor or nobleman.

The daughters of the imperial court and of provincial nobles were also 'educated', although not so formally in a school, rather in the houses of Cuzco noblewomen.

Right: Face markings, an elaborate hat and earrings, and a poised kero *cup in this Chancay anthropomorphic ceramic vessel possibly indicate that the girl is participating in a libation ritual.*

MARRIAGE AND INHERITANCE

Inca marriage was normally monogamous. Such an arrangement was not, however, a legal or social obligation, rather an economical one. A man could have more than one wife but only if he had sufficient wealth to support them and their children. Nobles often took several wives, and the Inca emperor could have as many wives as he wanted. In a glimpse of pre-Inca practice, the tale of Naymlap, founder of the northern coastal dynasty of the Lambayeque culture, mentions among his 'noble company' his wife, Ceterni, and a harem. The wives of some of his sons are also named.

CHOOSING PARTNERS

Inca emperors had the pick of the *aclla* (or *acllyaconas*) 'chosen women' from the cult of the 'Virgins of the Sun', and could also use the chosen women as favours and in marriage alliances with other rulers.

If a man had more than one wife, there was always a distinction between a principal wife and any secondary wives. The distinction was established in the formal

Below: Terracotta figurines of a couple wearing headdresses and with pectorals and earplugs, holding cups, Chancay culture.

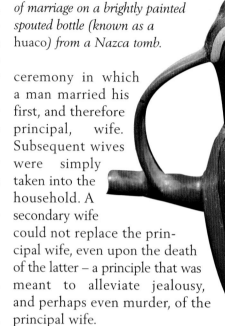

Right: Exemplifying the ancient union of marriage on a brightly painted spouted bottle (known as a huaco) *from a Nazca tomb.*

ceremony in which a man married his first, and therefore principal, wife. Subsequent wives were simply taken into the household. A secondary wife could not replace the principal wife, even upon the death of the latter – a principle that was meant to alleviate jealousy, and perhaps even murder, of the principal wife.

IMPERIAL BLOODLINES

In the imperial line, because the Incas believed the imperial *ayllu* had ultimately been founded by, and was therefore descended from, Inti (the sun god), the emperor was considered to be divine. To keep the imperial bloodline pure for purposes of ascent to the throne, therefore, the emperor was also required to have one official wife, the *coya*, who was supposed to be his full sister. The heir to the throne, chosen by the reigning emperor, was selected from the children of their union. The children of the emperor's secondary wives formed the *panacas* (royal *ayllus*). Marriages within non-royal *ayllus* were not obliged to be to sisters because no question of divinity or pureness of descent was involved.

Despite these theoretical 'rules' or laws of imperial descent, by the 12th–13th generations of Inca rulers, the succession of the death of Huayna Capac (twelfth emperor) was disputed by two half-brothers, Huáscar and Atahualpa, from different imperial wives.

One other curious Inca elite marriage custom was the pairing of noble couples. One Inca source claimed that marriageable young men and women of the highest nobility lined up annually in the main plaza in Cuzco, whereupon the emperor selected pairs and formally married them. It would seem safe to conjecture that pairs lined up such that pre-arranged or hoped-for matches could be achieved.

WIFELY DUTIES

One of the main duties of the secondary wives in a large household was to act as child-carers for the legitimate sons of their husband, both their own sons and the sons of the principal wife. When these sons reached puberty, one duty of the secondary wife was to teach him about sex, including having intercourse with him, although presumably not with her own sons.

And when such a son married, the secondary wife remained in his household and continued with the duties of a secondary wife.

Such complicated arrangements were not the norm among the bulk of Andean society. Inca marriage was usually within one's *ayllu*, as this practice maintained the existing rights, property and obligations of the collective. Related families usually lived near each other in their *suyu* quarters, divided into their two moieties. A woman normally moved into her husband's *suyu* and moiety, but remained a member of her ancestral moiety and lineage. Inheritance was both through the male and female lines. This 'gender parallelism' represents an aspect of the fundamental Andean concept of duality. Men traced their ancestry and birthrights through their fathers, while women traced theirs through their mothers.

MARRIAGE RITES

The marriage ceremony incorporated and ritualized this gender equality between husband and wife. Marriage agreements and arrangements were made either by a

couple's parents or by the couple themselves. The ancestral *mallquis* mummies were often consulted on the suitability of the match, although how their opinion was determined is uncertain. The usual age for marriage was about 25 years for men and between 16 and 20 for women.

The marriage ceremony was simple, if formal. The groom, accompanied by his family, went to the bride's house, where he was greeted and his bride formally presented to him. The groom's family signalled their acceptance of the girl by placing a sandal on her foot – a wool sandal if she was a virgin and a grass sandal if she was not. (Virginity was not a requirement of marriage, although the Spanish sources give no information about how virginity, or otherwise, was determined.)

Left: Chimú polished black bridge-spout bottle showing a domestic scene of a woman with braided hair holding her baby.

Above: Moche potters were not shy of depicting old age, as on this stirrup-spouted bottle of an elderly couple embracing.

Next, both families travelled to the groom's home. His bride presented him with gifts, and the elders of the two families expounded to the couple on the many duties and responsibilities of family life. Once these sober rituals were completed, the wedding was celebrated with a feast and the presentation of gifts to the newlyweds by family members. As a formal acknowledgement of the reciprocal relationship being established in this first stage of marriage, between both the marrying couple and their respective lineages, the bride's parents often signified their agreement by accepting a gift of coca from the groom's parents.

Divorce was not recognized in Inca law, and a man who cast aside his wife was punished and required to take her back.

GENDER ROLES

In the earliest times, we can only surmise and use the example of hunter-gatherer societies of today to reconstruct gender roles. Game-hunting must have been predominantly a male pursuit; gathering while tending children a female role. Coastal cultures, for example, probably combined these occupations seamlessly as men fished and hunted sea mammals from small boats offshore while woman and children gathered shellfish along the foreshore.

However, it is too easy to slip into this apparent 'obvious' division of labour. If children participated in gathering, they would have included both boys and girls, at least up to a certain age. The necessary collection and preparation of materials for building shelters must have been a combined effort by both men and women.

Below: Spinning and weaving were a continuous task for Inca women. As well as the more mobile backstrap loom, large textiles were made on horizontal single-heddle looms.

Similarly, there is no reason to think that spiritual matters – shamanism, divining and soliciting the gods, and medicinal and herbal practices – were the exclusive realm of one gender or the other. In early times of basic survival, roles must have been more mixed, and the group effort as a whole was the most important factor.

Before Inca conquest and their institutionalization of life, gender roles were less fixed. In Inca society, male and female roles became more defined, especially in the primary conception that men were soldiers and women were cloth makers. The elite classes had servants and personal attendants to make life easier, but elite men still served as soldiers in the imperial army and elite women still spun and wove to demonstrate their respective masculinity and femininity.

Spanish sources say more about men's roles than women's, especially about men's obligations under *mit'a* labour, as craftsmen and in the imperial court.

Above: Both men and women performed tasks in the fields. Here men turn the soil with foot-ploughs while women crush the sods into finer soil (depicted in Poma de Ayala's Nueva Corónica, *c.1615).*

MEN'S ROLES

The principal role fulfilled by men in the Inca Empire was their obligation of tax. All taxpaying individuals, that is heads of households, were required to provide someone to work for a certain period of time each year in the state *mit'a* labour system. Inca practice was formalized, but there is every reason to believe that the system was not wholly invented by the Incas.

Evidence from pre-Inca coastal and highland cultures indicates that labour levies were employed for major communal constructions. The makers' marks on the adobe bricks of the Moche Huaca del Sol show that the monument was built by organized gangs of workers using some system of state regimentation of the workforce. Similarly, the regimented nature of Wari architecture indicates that the labour forces that built them were marshalled on a regular basis as and when additions were built at the capital city, provincial cities and fortresses.

The Inca *mit'a* required men to discharge various roles, depending on their individual skills. A man could be drafted into the army, or he could be employed in road and bridge building, or other state constructions. He could serve as an administrator in the state redistribution system, or be a transporter of food and goods to and from them. If he was a skilled craftsman, his services might be employed in the production of metalwork or ceramics for the state. A large proportion of *mit'a* labour was used to work the lands or to tend the llama flocks designated for the support of the imperial and elite households, and of religious cults.

WOMEN'S ROLES

Women were typically in charge of the household. In common households, women performed the principal tasks of child rearing, especially when children were young, and were responsible for preparing meals, cleaning, washing and making cloth and clothing for the family. When old enough, children contributed to household activities. At this time, boys' and girls' roles differentiated and they began to take on traditional gender roles.

A particular role fulfilled by women in Inca and pre-Inca society was spinning and weaving. Cotton was the predominant fibre in the lowlands and wool in the highlands. Spinning was done with a drop spindle and therefore enabled women to spin thread almost anywhere and while otherwise preoccupied. For example, when simply walking between tasks it was possible to keep the spindle whorl in motion while feeding cotton or wool to it from a ball in the hand.

The importance of cloth and the persistent demand for it by the Inca state bureaucracy meant that all women span and wove, from the humblest citizen to the women of the imperial household. Women also played a significant role in religion, one special role being life in the imperial cult of 'chosen women', the *acllas* (or *acllyaconas*). Women also played the principal role tending the temple and in the cult of the Moon.

Left: Service in battle was a principal obligation of Inca men and also in much earlier empires – as shown by this Moche warrior with shield and war club as a stirrup-spouted pot.

Above: Small gardens for growing gourds and herbs and other condiments were tended near the household. The man is offering coca leaves to the woman (note the early adoption of European chickens); depicted in Poma de Ayala's Nueva Corónica, *c.1615.*

COMMUNAL TASKS

On lands designated for the support of commoners, both men and women performed the planting, care and harvest of crops. Hunting and fishing remained men's work, although shellfish collection probably remained a task for women and children.

The nature of *ayllu* kinship ties and obligations shows that much of farm labour and local building activities such as irrigation canals and house-building was accomplished by the combined efforts of men and women, each having roles in the preparation and use of the various materials and tasks involved.

Members of the imperial Inca court and other elite society had an easier life. They could draw upon the resources of private estates and *mit'a* tribute. (They were themselves, of course, exempt from *mit'a* obligations.) Noblemen could also fill command positions in the Inca army or serve as officials in state administrative positions. Priestly positions were also open to them.

CLOTHING AND HAIRSTYLES

People's clothing and hairstyles established their ethnic identity. Among a tribe or nation, differences in style and quality of clothing and jewellery indicated social rank and status. In Andean creation, Viracocha made figurines and painted them with the costumes and hairstyles of different nations. In his wanderings, he assigned distinctive clothing, hairstyles and languages as he called forth peoples and nations from the Earth.

INCA DAILY WEAR

Ordinary Incas wore simple clothing. Women wrapped a large cloth around the body, pinned at the shoulders and tied with a belt at the waist. A mantle was draped over the shoulders and fastened at the front with a large copper pin (*tupu*). Thickened thighs and ankles, considered by Incas a special attribute of feminine beauty, were enhanced by tying string above and below the knees.

Men wore a loincloth wrapped around the waist and groin and a cloth tunic over the body. The tunic comprised a

Below: This tunic of fine alpaca wool, with its elaborate interlocking geometric designs and stylistic feline and crab motifs, would have been worn by a nobleman, and perhaps accompanied him to his tomb.

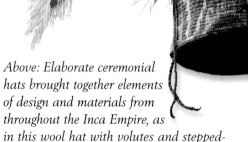

Above: Elaborate ceremonial hats brought together elements of design and materials from throughout the Inca Empire, as in this wool hat with volutes and stepped-fret designs, and tropical feather adornment.

large cloth folded double and sewn together, leaving slits for the head and arms. Men covered their legs from knee to ankle with wraps of cotton or wool fringes. In the cold, they wore long capes over their shoulders.

Despite its simple design, clothing was usually decorated with symbolic, brightly coloured patterns. Ordinary daywear was decorated with a single band of square designs around the waist and along the lower edge, plus an inverted triangle at the neck. Designs on men's clothing were standardized to signify membership of a particular group – distinct for his *ayllu* or as a member of one of the royal *panacas*.

Footwear for both men and women was sandals, secured with woollen straps tied across the foot. Commoners wore sandals woven from wild plant fibres, or of cotton, llama or alpaca wool. Soles were leather (deer or other animal hide).

HATS

Both men and women wore headdresses, the shapes of which were, in addition to cloth decoration, indicators of ethnic identity. Inca men wore cloth headbands. Hats were conical or flared cloth pieces, with elite versions being decorated with cloth and metalwork tassels and feathers. Nazca burials include elite individuals with tall, feathered headpieces, revealing wealth and long-distance contacts with sources of brightly coloured tropical bird feathers. Nazca figures on pottery and figurines wear tight, rectangular 'hats', perhaps representing the cloth turbans (wrapped around and over the head with the ends tied in front) found on Nazca mummies.

Moche people wore a variety of helmet-like headpieces. Examples of Wari and Tiwanaku hats are blocky, often cube-shaped, and sometimes have cloth horns at the corners. But such headgear is probably the elaborate wear of ritual, for priests and nobles, rather than common wear.

STYLES AND DISTINCTIONS

There was little difference in style between commoner and elite; quality and quantity were the main distinctions – the cut of the cloth and its fineness, the amount of jewellery and other accoutrements, and the decorative elaboration and materials used. Whereas common *tupus* were copper, nobles used silver and gold ones. Inca and other nobles wore feather headdresses and crowns of silver and gold. Nobles

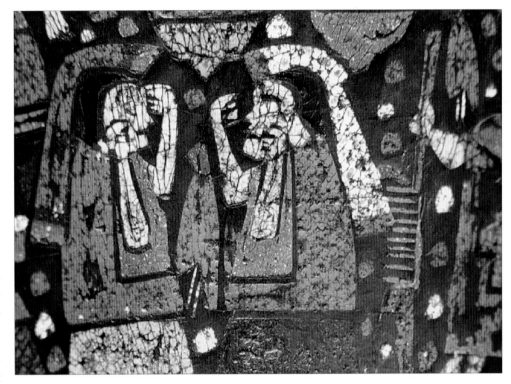

attached gold and silver ornaments to their sandals, and Inca emperors wore non-functional silver or gold sandals; copper and gold sandals were also found in earlier elite Moche and Lambayeque-Sicán burials.

The Inca emperor's headband was long enough to wrap several times around his head and only he could wear a headband decorated with a fringe of tassels that hung over his forehead, and carry a stick with a dangling pompom.

Inca imperial and other heads of state, and priests, wore clothes cut from the finest textiles, dyed with the richest colours. Only they had access to exotic fibres, such as alpaca and vicuña wool, tropical bird feathers and embellishments of gold and silver thread. Inca elites were especially fond of tropical feather decorations: mantles

were sometimes covered entirely in feathers, or in gold, silver or copper discs, to emphasize high social status.

PRE-INCA CLOTHING

Inca clothing and jewellery reflects what was worn in earlier cultures. The fine clothes and featherwork of the Lords of Chimór (Chimú) are especially notable. The elaborate wraps of Paracas and Nazca burials and the costumes worn by figures on pottery, murals, metalwork and stone sculpture must be viewed with caution regarding everyday wear. Much of the special cloth and headgear in burials is costume for special occasions – burials, ritual ceremony or battle gear – or is worn by representations of deities. Interestingly, Viracocha (Creator) is described as wearing a simple, rough cloak or even rags!

SPECIAL COSTUME

More elaborate, special costumes, styled on the themes described above, were made for special ritual occasions.

Left: As well as garments, llama wool and elaborate patterns were applied to utilitarian accessories, such as this Inca coca leaf bag with opposing rows of llama figures.

Above: Distinctive ceremonial costumes are also known from decorations on objects, as on this painted kero cup showing priests or priestesses in ritual dress and headgear.

Jewellery was worn mostly by nobles. Inca women wore *tupus* and necklaces. Men wore little or no jewellery, but the insignia of Inca nobility was the large earplugs given at puberty. These were round, about 5cm (2in) in diameter and held by a shaft through the earlobe. They were made of copper, silver, gold or metal alloy, or stone. Men also wore metal bracelets.

Men who showed particular bravery in battle were awarded metal discs to wear around the neck. They often donned necklaces of the teeth of their human victims. The Incas also painted their faces in mourning, and Inca warriors wore warpaint into battle.

HAIRSTYLES

Inca hairstyles were simple: men cut their hair short and bound it by a cloth headband, whereas women grew it long with a central parting. A woman cut her hair only in mourning or as a sign of disgrace. An Inca girl grew her hair throughout childhood, for at the onset of puberty it was braided by her mother on the fourth day after her first menstruation, as one of the signs of her transition to adulthood.

CRIME AND PUNISHMENT

Inca life was highly regimented, both because the general necessity to make a living took up most of people's time, and because the state regulated most activity in some way or other. Such must have been the case in pre-Inca cultures as well. There would consequently *seem* to have been little crime as we know it.

THE LAW

There was, however, Inca law, and pre-Inca societies undoubtedly had social rules, the transgression of which, if discovered, entailed punishment of some sort by the state or by one's peers. No archaeological evidence can be definitively ascribed to a crime or punishment. Even the gruesome treatment of the individuals in some Nazca graves seems to be religiously motivated rather than owing to criminal punishment. (At Cahuachi some men, women or children had their mouth pinned by cactus spines or tongue removed and placed in a pouch, or had their eyes blocked, their skull perforated for threading on a cord, or even excrement inserted into the mouth.)

There is a hint of such control, inevitably involving religion, however, in the famous tale of Fempellec, the

Left: Punishment for crime was scaled not only according to the crime, but also according to social rank – the higher your rank the more severe your punishment. Plucking out an eye was one punishment for treason (from Poma de Ayala's Nueva Corónica, *c.1615).*

ambitious twelfth descendant of the conquering king Naymlap of the northern coastal valleys. Fempellec attempted to remove the greenstone idol of the state dynastic god Yampallec from the capital Chot to another city. The cult priests, however, heartily disapproved of this sacrilegious act. A demon appeared (conjured up by the priests?) in the form of a beautiful woman, who seduced Fempellec – an act that caused 30 days of rain followed by a year of drought and the inevitable crop failures and famine. In retribution the priests seized and bound Fempellec, then threw him into the sea and left him to drown. Such rough justice probably represents a moral tale about what respect is owed to the gods and the consequences

Above: Incarceration was one option for crime: the so-called prison buildings at Machu Picchu, possibly also used to hold noble captives for ransom.

that can be expected if they are not honoured. The gods wreaked punishment on the people, and the priests exercised their punishment on the person responsible for the 'crime'.

APPLICATION OF LAW

Inca civil law applied to various social and state activities. Pachacuti Inca Yupanqui (tenth emperor, 1438–71) is credited by Garcilasco de la Vega with having set down basic Inca law, including punishments for blasphemy, patricide, fratricide, homicide, treason, adultery, child-stealing, seduction, theft and arson. Inca law governed tribal rights and obligations to the empire, the division of land and other property, the system of work rotation and the *mit'a* tax system. (The basic laws were few: laziness, lying, stealing, murder and adultery were crimes.) It also applied to

Above: Pachacuti Yupanqui, tenth Sapa Inca, is credited with setting out the basic Inca laws in the 15th century after his successful defence of Cuzco and defeat of the Chancas (oil on canvas, 18th-century 'Peruvian School').

It was rare for an Inca citizen or subject to be without the basic necessities of life. Therefore maltreatment of the elderly or disabled, to whom one would owe obligations in the *ayllu* kinship system, would be harshly dealt with.

Divorce was not recognized. A husband who cast aside his wife was forced to take her back; doing so again brought public whipping; a third time meant execution by clubbing or being thrown off a cliff.

Treason was punished by imprisonment, which almost always resulted in death. The traitor was thrown into an underground cell filled with venomous snakes and dangerous animals in Cuzco.

In addition to the basic laws of the land, the Inca emperor was entitled to enact new laws to suit his needs and new occasions. For example, Pachacuti is credited with decreeing that only princes and their sons could wear gold, silver and precious stone ornaments, multicoloured feather plumes or vicuña wool.

Below: Adultery was a serious crime: commoners were tortured, as depicted here by Poma de Ayala, c.1615; nobles who committed adultery were put to death.

proper conduct as an adult and as a married man or woman and the treatment of others, including the support of the elderly and disabled.

PUNISHMENT

There was a different punishment for every crime; but the punishment meted out to the perpetrator was scaled according to his or her social rank: the higher the status of the individual, the more severe the punishment. For example, although virginity was not a requirement of marriage, adultery by a commoner was punished by torture. But if a noblewoman committed adultery, both parties of the crime were put to death. A common punishment was beating with a stone club, sometimes to death. Other methods of execution were to be thrown off a cliff, or to be hung over a ravine by the hair until the roots gave way. A slovenly housewife was made to eat the household dirt; a husband who did not keep a tidy house had to eat dirt or drink his family's dirty bath water. Laziness was punished by whipping; chronic laziness by death.

CAPITAL PUNISHMENT

In a state that so highly regulated the collection and redistribution of property (the foodstuffs and materials produced under state organization), it was inevitable that a crime against the government was dealt with especially severely. Stealing from fields, whether they were state, religious or commoners' lands, was punishable by death. The same applied to theft from llama herds or from state storehouses.

MUSIC, DANCE AND RECREATION

We do not know what ancient Inca or pre-Inca music sounded like. The Peruvian or Andean panpipe music that became popular in the latter half of the 20th century cannot be taken as representative of pre-Hispanic Andean music for two reasons. First, accompanying guitars, and probably the harp, are post-Spanish Conquest introductions; second, new rhythms, melodies and musical concepts from European and other cultures have inevitably influenced it in the 500 years since the Spanish Conquest.

There is undoubtedly some continuity, however. The so-called Peruvian panpipes have an ancient Andean history and thus at least physical continuity. Andean rhythms are also distinctly different from Western European cadences, and might also reflect continuity. But we have no written examples of Andean music, so cannot be certain.

THE INSTRUMENTS

Archaeologists have found examples of instruments dating from at least the Early Horizon. There are Paracas and Nazca flutes, resembling modern recorders. Flutes were the only instrument in general use throughout the Andes. Panpipes comprise joined pottery or cane flutes of different lengths to produce different notes and tones. Ancient pottery examples differ from modern panpipes in that they have closed ends; thus sound is produced by blowing across the tops rather than through them.

Seashell trumpets were also used, different sizes and shapes producing haunting single tones. Moche pots, for example, depict figures blowing conch trumpets. Among the entourage of the legendary Naymlap is one Fonga Sigde, 'Blower of the Shell Trumpet'. Finally, there was a variety of percussion instruments: drums, tambourines, bells, rattles, and clackers of animal bone and wood.

THE ROLE OF MUSIC

Ancient Andean music and dance appears to have been predominantly for ceremony, played at special occasions for specific purposes, rather than as pure entertainment, although they undoubtedly gave participants and onlookers pleasure. Music formed a central role in Nazca ritual, as depicted on wall paintings at Cahuachi. Ritual processions along Nazca line figures were probably accompanied by flutes, drums, bells and trumpets.

Moche music appears to have been primarily associated with religion, sacrifice and war. Moche pots frequently

Left: A Chimú bottle with a group of musicians around the spout, showing a panpipe player flanked by two percussionists with gourd drums.

Above: Music and dance were frequently portrayed by the Moche in pottery, as here in this flute player effigy stirrup-spout bottle.

depict groups of musicians – principally flute, trumpet and drum players – as part of ritual combat and sacrifice scenes, and shamanism. Copper, gold and silver bells were attached to the metal plates covering the body of the Sipán Lord burial, and the accompanying burial of one of his ritual assistants was evidently a panpipe musician. The Moche associated the peanut with flute-playing.

Moche flutes and rattles in the handles of ritual vessels were for trance-inducement. Drums were used in religious ritual, and may also have been used to set a pace for weaving – a drum was found in the Pampa Grande textile workshop.

Inca music accompanied dance at festivals and initiation rites. It was also important in 'entertaining' labourers who worked on Inca engineering and agricultural projects. Gifted individuals were also trained as royal court musicians, and it is recorded that some players played several flutes together to extend the sound range. Flutes were also used for love songs, and drums, trumpets and flutes accompanied Inca armies on the march.

STRANGE MUSIC

Curiously, some Late Horizon Chimú double-chambered vessels, the two parts connected by a bridge, produced a whistle. The liquid level in the chambers changes tone, which escapes from a hole at the top of one chamber.

The tonal qualities of water for religious inspiration were also appreciated at Chavín de Huantár. Running gushing water around the interior conduits of the chambers of its labyrinthine temple produced an awesome roar from the door (mouth) of the temple that was heard by the assembled worshippers in the courtyard outside.

THE DANCE

Inca dancing was restricted to ritual occasions: seasonal festivals in the agricultural year, to accompany religious ceremony,

and at life-stage recognition. The idea of social dancing did not exist. Such was undoubtedly the purpose of dance in pre-Inca cultures as well.

Inca dance was formal, with participants performing a series of specific movements in unison. Special dances were performed by men (for example at puberty rites), and women (for example at harvesting rituals); other dances involved both sexes. When *mallquis* mummies were brought out to participate in the ceremony, songs and dances were performed before them, and stories of their exploits recited.

RECREATION

Almost nothing is known about ancient Andean 'leisure' activities, probably because there was little time for anything other than the necessary daily tasks. Even ritual dancing, singing and music were considered essential for life and wellbeing rather than recreation or entertainment. Children began to fulfil daily tasks as soon as they were capable.

Chicha beer drinking on ritual and ceremonial occasions could obviously *de facto* become 'recreational'.

Left: Drums made of wood, pottery, gourds and stretched hide were also common instruments for ritual and dance ceremonies. This Moche stirrup-spout bottle is in the shape of a drummer with his bone or wooden beater, his hat held with a chin strap.

Above: Various pipes and flutes were the most common instruments. Sets of pitched panpipes were made of both pottery and reeds bound with twine or decorated textiles, such as these Nazca examples.

Inca children played with balls and tops and at games using rounded pottery pieces for markers and counters. Adults played a dice game with five, rather than six, numbers. There were also board games that used bean counters. The Incas also gambled, often for high stakes. Inca nobles played a game called *aylloscas*, in which entire estates were wagered. We do not know the rules for any of these games.

Warfare being so important in Inca society, boys were 'trained' in games of skill intended to test them and make them brave and tough. There were races and mock battles that were taken with such seriousness that severe injuries are recorded.

Nothing is known of recreation in pre-Inca cultures, except perhaps the ritual combat of the Moche, in which individuals had lifetime careers. This was a deadly profession, however, for religious purposes and sacrifice.

By Inca times, hunting was mostly recreational. It broke the monotonous routine of agriculture, and also had the outcome of providing meat. Hunting by Inca and provincial noblemen was surely recreation for them.

DEATH AND BURIAL

Death in the Andean world was not considered the end of existence: it was the next stage or state of being after life on Earth. Archaeological evidence of elite and common burials shows that elaborate preparations were made, almost throughout life, for this next state of being. Moreover, the Andean worldview applied this belief to all living things – humans, animals and plants – and to the Earth itself as a 'living' entity.

LIKE A PLANT
Anthropologist Frank Salomon describes the Andean outlook on life's cycle as a "pervasive vegetative metaphor". Plants provide a metaphor for human and animal life as they progress from tender shoots through firmer, resilient stems and plants, then mature, rigid, but drier plants, and finally to a desiccated state – just as humans progress from newborns, through infanthood, puberty, young adulthood, old age, and death, though enduring as mummies. The mummified body was likened to a dried pod from which seeds of new life dropped.

ELITE AND COMMON
Burial and afterlife, however, varied throughout Andean civilization. The greatest contrast is in the treatment of elite members of society and common people. The rich burials of nobles and priests in Moche-Sipán and Lambayeque-Sicán tombs and the elaborate burials of some Nazca dead, for example, contrast with simpler interments in common graves with a few tools and pots.

PRESERVING THE BODY
The Initial Period Chinchorros and La Paloma peoples of the Chilean coast show attempts to preserve the actual flesh in addition to the soul or essence of 'life'.

Above: A Nazca mummy bundle, the final wrapping being a plain woven shroud bound with cord.

In the Early Horizon and Early Intermediate Period, the unfinished states of some Paracas and Nazca mummy textile wraps show that they were being prepared long before, and in anticipation of, physical death. Paracas and Nazca elaborate burial procedures show that considerable care and planning were involved. Nevertheless, burial in tombs removed the bodies from the living. Ancestor worship or honour was evident in these cultures, as demonstrated by the care of burial and by the fact that most tombs were reopened periodically to place other kin members inside.

Left: A bulky Paracas mummy bundle with effigy face and feathered cap – the higher your rank, the more elaborate the bundle and textile patterns.

Above: On the southern Peruvian coast, the Nazca are noted for deep, mud-brick-lined tombs, ancestral vaults, which they reopened for successive burials through generations.

them. Late Intermediate Period people in the Titicaca Basin placed their mummies in special burial towers – *chullpas* – as sepulchres meant to be reopened periodically for the deposit of other mummies.

Other cultures, however, treated their mummies differently. Chimú mummies of deceased rulers were housed in their own compounds, within a virtual city of the dead, within a city of the living. Each compound housed a living retinue to look after the dead ruler's remains, perform rituals respecting it, and collect food and other goods for daily life.

Inca mummies were kept very much as a part of the lives of the living. They were visited regularly and brought out on ritual occasions. They were consulted for advice, honoured with recitals of poetry and stories, and even 'fed' on ritual occasions.

PACARINA

Andean cultures believed that the essence of a dead person ultimately went to a final resting. The physical body was only a vessel for this life – the person's 'vital force', or soul, found its way to *pacarina*. *Pacarina* was the place of origin of one's ancestors and the ultimate source of rebirth. It could be a tree, rock, cave, spring or lake – a magical shelter from the world's ravages.

There were different names for *pacarina*. The people of Collasuyu and Cuntisuyu called it Puquina Pampa and Coropuna. Documents from Cajatambo call it Uma Pacha; and the peoples of the Lima region called it Upaymarca. Coastal peoples named the 'Island of Guano' as the final resting place.

Of common belief was a final resting place of farms, where the dead sowed their seeds. The spirit continued to tend the fields and crops, and to experience thirst and hunger as the body does on Earth, and so was fed by the living with offerings of food and drink. Those still living nevertheless also considered the spirits

of the dead to be dangerous. It was thus necessary to help the dead person's soul reach the end of its journey, lest the spirit wander among the living causing violence, sickness and accidents.

SACRIFICE

Death by ritual sacrifice was a special form of death and burial that was practised throughout Andean civilization. Human and animal sacrifices were performed to honour and supplicate the gods, commemorate the building of temples to them and appease the forces of nature. Decapitation, bludgeoning and strangulation were common.

Moche ritual combat was a special form of sacrificial death, as was the Inca practice of sacrifice and burial on remote high mountaintops. Another Inca practice was deliberate exposure to lightning, and if killed by it, burial of the *qhaqha* (lightning victim) at the place of death.

Below: Ancestral sepulchres were common in Andean cultures from early times. The Collao are famous for their stone chullpa towers, one group of which is at Sillustani near Puno, Lake Titicaca.

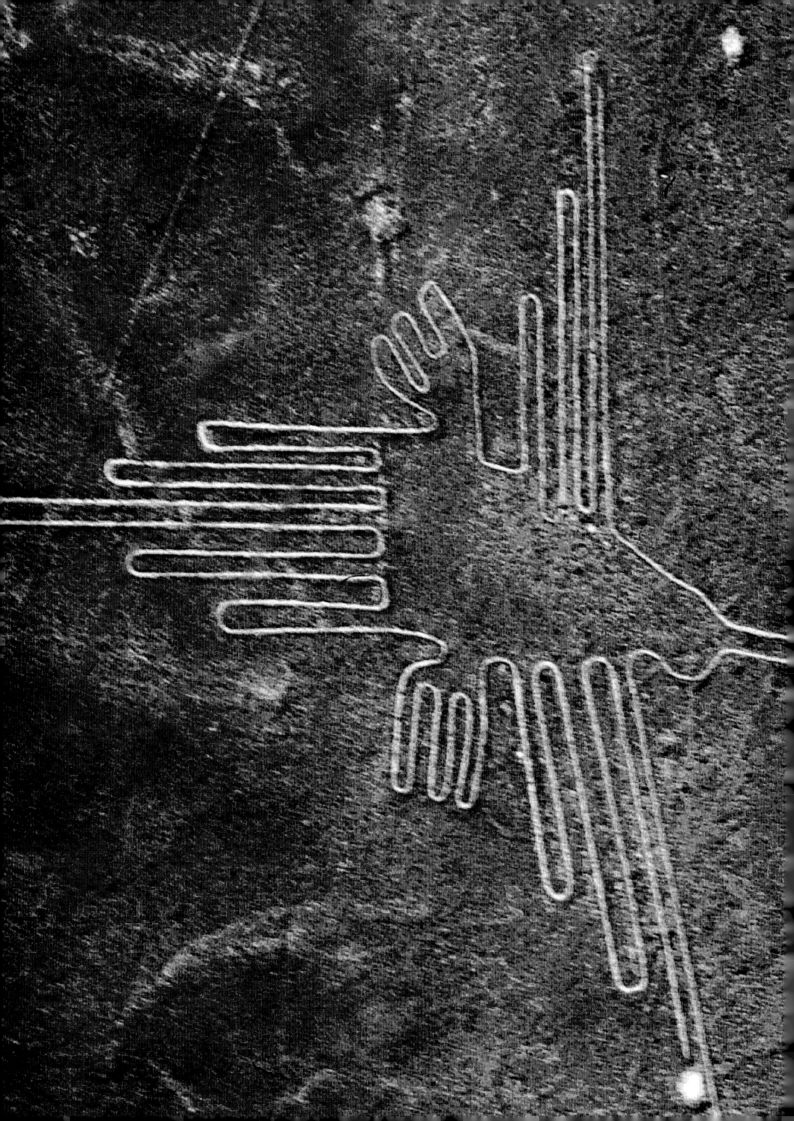

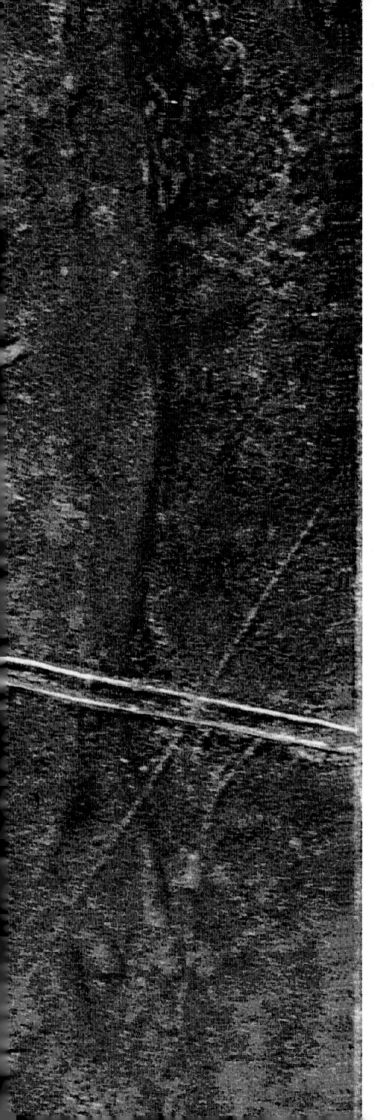

CHAPTER SIX

RELIGIOUS BELIEFS

Ancient Andeans' cosmogony and cosmology – their stories of how the world came into being and how it worked – helped them cope with the events of everyday life and with the periodic stress they faced in what was to them a sometimes unpredictable environment. The ancient Greek word *cosmeo* means 'to order or arrange', and incorporates the idea of 'good order'. Not surprisingly, then, ancient Andean mythical explanations of their cosmos and its origins put them in good order.

Astronomical observations, especially of the sun, moon and Milky Way, revealed to ancient Andeans a regular relationship between solar and lunar cycles and the seasons. Their observations enabled them to create a calendar, regulate their religious ceremonies and plan their work. Irregularities, such as natural disasters, were less understood because they appeared to be unpredictable. They were regarded as punishment by the gods for wrongdoing.

The gods created the world and divided it into its parts: the world of the living (the Inca *Kai Pacha*), the world above (*Hanan Pacha*) and the world below (*Uku Pacha*). Overseeing all was a supreme god or being (with various names, the two most common being Viracocha and Pachacamac), and a large pantheon of other deities. This world worked and was in good order because the gods made it so. The reciprocal part to be played by humans, in order to keep the world in good order, was proper deference to and worship of the gods.

Left: Symbolism and ritual pathways were a hallmark of ancient Andean religion, as in this Nazca hummingbird geoglyph.

BELIEF SYSTEMS AND LITERATURE

Without the favour of the gods, life could be difficult. At a daily level, religion permeated every aspect of Andean life. Thought about how the world was created and humans' place within it is evident in early burials, within which everyday items were included, presumably in the belief that the buried person would need them in some sort of afterlife. The careful treatment of bodies, attempting to preserve them, or to clothe and prepare them for burial in other special ways, shows that a belief in an afterlife had developed in Chinchorros, La Paloma, Paracas and other early cultures, and continued into Inca times.

RISE AND INCREASING COMPLEXITY

Religious beliefs became formalized alongside an increasing complexity in social and political organization. Imagery of deities representing the forces of nature and creation increased as religion developed its own organizational status within the state. A separate hierarchy of

Below: The Chincha in coastal Peru, one of many Inca conquests, had a shrine at La Centinella, a characteristic adobe brick temple mound forming the focus of an urban ceremonial centre.

individuals became dedicated to looking after the appeasement of the gods as intermediaries between the deities and the common people. Elaborate histories, now called mythology, developed as accepted explanations of how the world came into being, how humans were created, and what constituted proper conduct towards the gods.

The gods controlled the forces of nature and were believed to be responsible for events that brought benefit and wellbeing to humans, as well as disaster and hardship. It was therefore believed necessary to plead with them and make special efforts to solicit their approval. Specialists with powers and status that enabled them to negotiate with the gods on behalf of humans had to be provided for. Their needs (or demands) became substantial. In the Inca Empire the produce from a third of all lands was given for the upkeep of the state religion.

PRIESTS AS INTERMEDIARIES

Priestly communication with the gods was through trance-like states, even shape shifting (it was believed), to solicit guidance and sacred favour; conducting ritual and sacrificial offerings (animal and human) to the gods; and making images of them in stone, pottery, wood and

Above: Many Andean beliefs in natural deities endure. A 20th-century Aymara couple here prepare offerings at the Huaca of Mount Illimani.

metal, which were housed as idols in special temples. Priests also gave instruction and guidance to individuals and groups at mass ceremonies through omens and oracles.

Ceremonies to honour the gods became increasingly elaborate as Andean civilization evolved. The course of the seasons, regulating daily and seasonal patterns of life and work, together with observations of the heavens and the regular movements of celestial bodies, fostered the development of a cycle of rituals performed on specific dates. These included the solstices and equinoxes, and were co-ordinated with human lifecycles through the stages of birth, childhood, initiation into adulthood and death.

SACRED PLACES AND SPACES

Natural and man-made sacred places were numerous and varied. Mountains, bodies of water, springs and the sky were all sacred in their own right. In them and on them the gods were thought to dwell or be embodied. The term *huaca* (Quechua) was applied to any sacred location – natural, man-made or a modified natural place – embodying the spirit of a deity, and where offerings were made: caves, islands, springs, outcrops of rock, mountains, a boulder or pile of stones, even a field in which a significant event took place. The term *apu* (literally 'lord' in Quechua) was used for sacred peaks in a land dominated by prominent volcanic cones.

Designating space and building special structures for ceremonial performances began early. A Y-shaped structure was built on one side of the village at Monte Verde some 14,800 years ago. It had a raised, sand and gravel floor and associated artefacts differentiating it from the ordinary houses. These included clay-lined braziers at the rear of the hut,

Below: Diagram of Yana Phuyu *(the 'Dark Cloud' constellations): animal shapes seen by Andean peoples in* Ch'aska Mayu, *the 'celestial river' of the Milky Way.*

medicinal plants and chewed leaves, seeds, hides, animal bones and apparent burnt offerings.

In time, all Andean cultures built large, elaborate structures and enclosures for ceremony and worship. Different forms were combined in ceremonial complexes within cities, or in the landscapes around them. There were raised mounds, pyramid-platforms for supporting temples; sunken courts (round, square or rectangular); labyrinthine buildings or complexes housing images of the gods; walled sacred compounds; and geoglyphs or designated routes laid out on the ground, such as the Nazca lines and figures, and Inca sacred *ceque* site lines and routes.

SACRED LITERATURE

The only ancient Andean literature known is Inca. However, the recurrence in Chimú and Inca culture of the story of the 'Revolt of the Objects' (graphically

Above: The Ponce Monolith at Tiwanaku, believed to be a petrified member of a former race of giants, is representative of Andean belief systems featuring successive ages of creation.

depicted in Moche murals at the Huaca de la Luna) reveals that this tale had been told for at least a millennium!

Inca literature was oral, and mostly dealt with religion and history. There were stories, legends, songs, poems and doctrines. Being passed down verbally, they were subject to variation and personal interpretation. Few examples survive because so little was recorded or translated by Spanish officials. On the contrary, they resolutely destroyed it as idolatrous.

There were four categories: religious prayers and hymns, dramatic histories or legends, narrative poems, and songs. Prayers and hymns praise the gods and goddesses. Only two dramatic pieces survive, as poor translations. Narrative poems, memorized for recital at public ceremonies, almost all concern religion and histories of the emperors. Dramatic pieces, also emphasizing religious themes, were performed at dances, recited by one or two 'actors' and a chorus. Poetry and song (the former set to music) were mostly love songs.

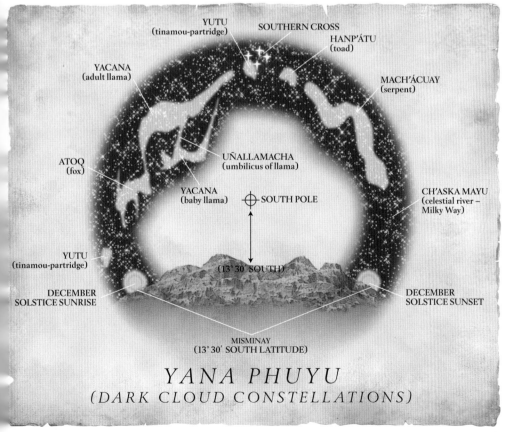

YACANA (adult llama)

YUTU (tinamou-partridge)

SOUTHERN CROSS

HANP'ÁTU (toad)

MACH'ÁCUAY (serpent)

ATOQ (fox)

UÑALLAMACHA (umbilicus of llama)

YACANA (baby llama)

SOUTH POLE

CH'ASKA MAYU (celestial river – Milky Way)

YUTU (tinamou-partridge)

(13° 30' SOUTH)

DECEMBER SOLSTICE SUNRISE

DECEMBER SOLSTICE SUNSET

MISMINAY (13° 30' SOUTH LATITUDE)

YANA PHUYU
(DARK CLOUD CONSTELLATIONS)

COMMON THEMES AND CONTINUITY

Religious beliefs about how the world worked were the enduring matrix that bound Andean civilization. Concepts that developed in Preceramic times continued, with cultural distinctiveness and elaboration, through to Inca times.

NATURAL AND RELIGIOUS CONTROLS

Ancient Andeans believed that natural forces were created and controlled by the gods. With so much of daily life and survival bound by the landscape, the ancient Andean worldview reflected the landscape by adhesion to it and through a sympathetic harmony with it.

Andean cities and, before true urbanization, the earliest ceremonial complexes of the Preceramic and Initial periods, maintained their relationship with the natural world not only through their physical configurations and economic viability but also through their religious institutions. Priests and shamans mediated society's ties to nature and relationships with the gods.

URBAN FOCUS

Ceremonial complexes and, later, religious precincts in cities were the focus for religious activities. Cities and buildings

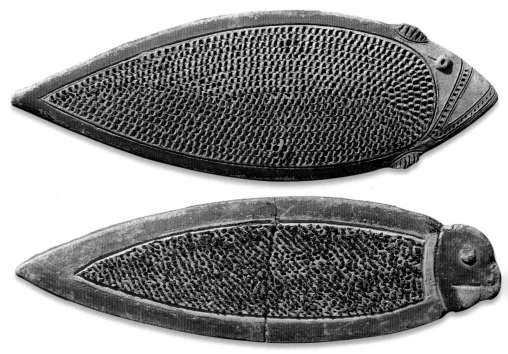

Above: Aquatic themes were common in Andean art, here exemplified by two fish carved from manioc (cassava) husks, La Tolita culture of Ecuador.

were oriented according to sacred concepts. Astronomical orientations sometimes guided routes and alignments. Temples and pyramid-platforms frequently faced sacred mountains, and sometimes even mimicked their contours

or profiles. Canals brought water to cities from holy springs. Even the plan of Cuzco, a crouching puma, honoured a revered animal.

Common architectural forms endured throughout ancient Andean history. The raising of tiered platform mounds began as early as 6000BC at Nanchoc in the Zana Valley. The combination of platforms and sunken courtyards, and the U-shaped configuration of temple complexes begun in Preceramic Period cultures, continued to the Late Horizon. Open plazas hosted large ritual gatherings, while enclosed courts were for more intimate worship. Sacred lines, predetermined pathways in the deserts and walled complexes, including sunken courts, controlled people's movements and directed them into ritual patterns. Windowless chambers and hidden passageways accommodated exclusive ritual and promoted mystery and power.

Left: Mount Parinacota, Chile: the permanence of the landscape was revered in the animism of mountains especially, each of which had its own huaca *or spiritual essence or was dwelt in or on by a deity.*

Open ceremonial space was juxtaposed by elements of hiddenness and obscurity: temple interiors and ceremonial compounds could be labyrinthine; oracles were housed in dark inner chambers; some ceremonies were performed by and for specialists only; sunken courtyards restricted numbers and obscured or regulated ritual.

These structures and activities were designed to ensure a proper relationship with the gods and nature. Offerings were made of the most precious objects, including the lives of animals and humans offered in dedication, honour and placation.

SUPREME BEINGS

A distinctive principal deity or creator being is recognizable in most cultures or regions. Mountain deities naturally predominated in highland cultures and sea gods in coastal valleys, yet early widespread contact between highlands, coasts and tropical forests spread more universal themes, even if imagery was culturally distinctive.

Below: Crustaceans were a common symbolic theme on Andean pottery and textiles. Here prawns are featured on a Nazca bridge-spout bottle.

The supreme deity at Chavín de Huántar, represented in the Staff Deity, was widespread in the Early Horizon, and could be male or female. The evolution of this supreme deity through several hundred years of the Chávin Cult incorporates combinations of feline, tropical cayman, serpentine and avian imagery.

Sky deities or attributes are common, and in addition to deities embodied in terrestrial features such as mountains or springs, the sun and the moon were commonly worshipped. The Moche supreme deity, often known as the Decapitator, features a rayed head, like the sun, and feline fangs. The Paracas–Nazca Oculate Being is distinctly celestial, depicted most frequently horizontally and with streaming appendages as if flying. Pachacamac, from his centre of worship in the city of Pachacamac, represented a supreme being with whom lesser deities throughout the Andean Area sought alliance through their priests. Official Inca religion simultaneously worshipped the supreme being Viracocha, the Creator, and promoted a state cult of the Sun (Inti), as well as worshipping other deities.

Above: The great Inti temple of Sacsahuaman was the ultimate sun temple and ceremonial precinct of Inca worship.

RELIGIOUS CEREMONY

People came to ancient Andean cities not for markets, as in other ancient civilizations, but for ritual. Special quarters housed craft workers who produced only luxury items and purpose-made ritual vessels destined for the elite, for offerings to the gods, and for burial. Annual cycles of ceremonies brought people into the cities in huge crowds during certain seasons. Elite goods, stored by the priestly and noble classes, were bestowed upon the celebrants on these occasions.

Regular ceremonies throughout the year were portrayed in art. Common animals and themes were depicted in all media and there was colour everywhere: in murals on temples and compound walls; on stone and wood sculptures; in polychrome ceramics and textiles for daily, ceremonial and funerary use; and in shimmering metalwork. Such imagery was a perpetual reminder to people of their religious obligations and need to solicit the favour of the gods.

Above: The great mud-brick temple mound at Moche, the Huaca de la Luna, forms a pair with the Huaca del Sol to honour two ancient fundamental Andean deities.

COMMON IMAGERY AND DUALITY

Ceremonial centre planning and common imagery developed in the Preceramic and Initial periods and became entrenched in the Early Horizon.

Widespread connections between coastal, highland and tropical forest cultures for exotic materials spread ideas and knowledge of plants and animals. Thus feline, serpentine and avian imagery became universal in the earliest textiles and later on in pottery and architectural sculptures. Insects, spiders, fish, and crustaceans and shellfish were also common themes. Composite beings, part-human/part-beast, were frequently portrayed as manifestations of deities, humans taking divine parts in ritual or humans in transformation under the influence of hallucinogenic substances.

Duality, with juxtaposed imagery and two-headed creatures, was commonly used in all media. From the Huaca Prieta twined double-headed crab and serpent cloth of *c.*2500BC, via the hawk and eagle images on the Black and White Portal columns at Chavín de Huántar's New Temple *c.*500BC, the male-female Yaya-Mama sculptures of the Titicaca Basin, the paired Tiwanaku, Wari and Inca gold figurines, and the two-faced Pachacamac idol to the twinned facing birds on a Chimú spondylus shell ornament, duality was a vital artery in Andean belief.

The use of hallucinogenic substances – another common religious practice – was believed to induce transformation, and is frequently depicted. Priests or shamans under the influence were believed to be able to gain insight regarding the cosmos and divine intentions, to take on the characteristics of revered animals such as a jaguar or raptor, and to heal the sick. Hallucinogenic trance was a means of temporarily departing this world and entering the 'other side' – yet another manifestation of duality.

Even economic and social structure reflect this concept, in the reciprocal trade relationships between highlands and lowlands and the division of kinship groups into two moiety groups: *hanan* (upper) and *hurin* (lower).

Right: The majestic condor, symbolic of the Andes, was sacred. Here a condor soars with extended talons on a Nazca bridge-spout bottle.

SACRIFICE

Sacrificial offerings to the gods solicited good weather and productive harvests, herding and fishing. They were also atonement to angry gods who caused natural disasters and El Niño weather cycles.

Human sacrifice frequently accompanied temple dedications and elite burials. From the sacrificed adult buried near the infant at Huaca de los Sacrificios at Preceramic Aspero, through the blood groove in the Lanzón Stela at Chavín de Huántar, the Moche and Tiwanaku decapitator deities, the mass grave behind the Huaca de la Luna at Moche and the 17 sacrificial victims in a Sicán tomb at Batán Grande, to Inca *capacocha* sacrifices, the taking of human (and animal) life pervaded Andean religion.

There was also a special cult of severed heads. At Preceramic Asia on the Peruvian central coast, eight severed heads were wrapped in a mat and ritually interred, while Nazca collectors perforated trophy head skulls and strung them on cords. Chavín de Huántar and Tiwanaku temple builders mounted stone-carved severed heads on plaza walls, and Inca warriors drank victory toasts from the skulls of slain opponents.

evident in the Chinchorros and La Palma cultures in southern Peru and northern Chile from c.5000BC. Efforts were made to preserve the body, and make it look alive with a wig and painted face.

Nazca tombs were periodically opened to deposit the bodies of generations of deceased, and the Cahuachi mound complex is thought to be a religious complex expressly for the mausoleums of kin groups from surrounding Nazca residential towns.

The ultimate in ancestor worship is exemplified in Chimú and Inca *mallquis* mummies. The preserved mummies of Chimú kings and Inca emperors and nobility, the founding members of kinship groups, were housed in elaborate settings. The core of the Chimú capital, Chan Chan, comprised vast walled compounds to house the dead rulers' mummies and their living retainers. Inca imperial *mallquis* were kept in special rooms in the sacred Coricancha temple. Virtually every Andean community in the Late Horizon had its *ayllu* ancestor mummies, stored in temples or in nearby sacred caves, to be brought out at religious rituals and consulted on communal and personal matters.

Above: A Moche portrait vessel, one of hundreds of individual portrait stirrup-spout bottle, shows a 'chief' – possibly a successful 'gladiator' – wearing a winged bird helmet.

ANCESTOR WORSHIP
Ancient Andean religious beliefs regarded 'being' as a perpetual cycle or revolution (*pachacuti* in Quechua). Death was considered a different state of being, in which the dead person entered another world and in some respects carried on in a life not dissimilar to the one departed on Earth.

Thus it was important to maintain links with the 'other side' through ancestor worship. Special preparation before burial is

RELIGIOUS TRADITIONS, PILGRIMAGE AND ORACLES
Religious continuity was secured in ancient Andean civilization through the early development of recognizable 'traditions'. The earliest of these are perhaps

the Kotosh Religious Tradition, exemplified by the successive Temple of the Crossed Hands and Temple of the Niches at Kotosh, and the Plazas Hundidas Tradition (hidden courts), both prevailing in the Preceramic and Initial periods.

Continuity and coherence in the Early Horizon was through religious belief rather than political unification. Two spheres, although not exclusive, focused on the Chavín Cult and Staff Deity in the northern and central Andes, and in the Pukará Yaya-Mama Cult of the Titicaca Basin.

Many early U-shaped ceremonial centres and Kotosh Tradition sites were centres for local communities. Whether their religious influence was more widespread because they were cult centres is open to debate. Later sites, such as Chavín de Huántar, Moche, Tiwanaku and Pachacamac, and imperial Inca Cuzco itself, were certainly cult and pilgrimage centres, recognized as such through analogy with the pilgrimage and oracle city of Pachacamac, which endured despite Wari, Inca and Spanish conquest and is thus described in chronicles.

Below: A whistle-spout/bridge-spout bottle of the Early Intermediate Period Vicus culture features crayfish on gourd bases and a feeding bird.

CREATION AND COSMOLOGY

Andean cosmological belief was 'organic'. The universe was regarded as an animate being, a living entity, rather than as a mechanical object. Celestial motions, the seasons and the ways the natural world functioned were ordered, and could be relied on. They believed that the universe was ordered, and thus showed design. But at the same time, it was believed to have been created by the gods and so was controlled by them.

CREATION AND CREATORS
Beliefs stemming from the forces of nature provided a common base from which later Andean cultures constructed elaborate stories of creation. Most included a great flood and the survival of

Left: One of the many stone stelae at Tiwanaku, believed to be the petrified bodies of a former race of giants.

Above: To many Andean cultures Tiwanaku and Lake Titicaca were the place of the origin of the world and of humans. Tiwanaku's Akapana temple mound and stellae, depicted here in 1845 by Alcides D'Obigny, was long a site of religious pilgrimage.

a single man and woman. Variations explain several stages of creation, in which the gods made the universe, the sun and moon, and perfected their design of humankind to make beings capable of worshipping them properly.

The two most important creator gods were Viracocha and Pachacamac. They were almost interchangeable as all-powerful gods, somewhat aloof and removed from day-to-day affairs, although Pachacamac was predominantly a coastal and lowland deity, while Viracocha predominated in the highlands.

VIRACOCHA AND THE BASIC STORY
The creation of the universe was thought to have taken place in the Titicaca Basin. Viracocha emerged from Lake Titicaca and made a dark world, without sun, moon or stars, and a race of giants. This race was to live peacefully and worship Viracocha, but instead it defied him. He turned some of the giants into stone; others were swallowed by the earth and sea. A great flood (*unu pachacuti*) swamped the land, drowning everything but one man and one woman, who landed at Tiwanaku.

Next Viracocha created the sun, moon and stars, and set them in motion from the Island of the Sun and Island of the Moon in the lake. He made a second, normal-sized human race from stone and clay, named them and painted them with their national costumes and hairstyles, then dispersed them underground in their future homelands. With two or three helpers he then travelled through the land, calling forth the nations to re-emerge through caves, and also from hills and lakes, as he went, until he reached the north-west coast and disappeared across the sea – in one version on a cloak raft, in another walking on the water.

THE FIVE AGES
An Inca version of creation, retold by Guaman Poma de Ayala, was of five ages of creation.

The first age was darkness. Its inhabitants, the *Wari Wiracocharuna*, were primitive, wore leaf clothing and ate 'unprocessed vegetal matter'. They worshipped Viracocha and Pachacamac, but they were later destroyed in an unspecified manner.

The second age had the more advanced race of the *Wari Runa* as its inhabitants. They wore animal skins, practised primitive agriculture and lived in peace, believing Viracocha to be their creator. Nevertheless, a great flood ended their existence.

The third age, inhabited by the *Purun Runa*, was civilized. People practised irrigation agriculture, span and dyed wool and cotton, made pottery and mined for metal to make jewellery. Each town had a ruler, but there was increased warfare as the population increased. Pachacamac was worshipped as the creator.

The *Auca Runa* inhabited the fourth age. Civilization and technology were more sophisticated in every regard. Conflict had increased to the point where people lived in fortified towns on hilltops. The social arrangements of *ayllu* kinship divisions and decimal administration came into being. It is not specified how this age ended.

The fifth age was that of the Incas and all they brought and created: imperial rule, *ayllus* and bipartite 'moiety' divisions of *hanan* (upper) and *hurin* (lower), and decimal bureaucracy. There were six principal gods, the most important being Viracocha, the Creator, and Inti, the Sun.

These creation stories, and many permutations of them, were meant to explain how the world came to be, why the gods were important and should be honoured, and how the technology and craftsmanship came into being. Guaman Poma de Ayala's version amounts to a potted history. The Incas became a repository for religious developments going back to the Preceramic Period. They embraced the multitudes of local deities and creation stories.

COSMOLOGY AND CALENDARS

The regularities of the seasons, the cycles of the sun, the phases of the moon and the progression of the Milky Way across the night sky were evidence of a plan, of a supreme intelligence who had created them and set them in motion – a being

Above The Wari Runa *were the second race of people in the Inca creation myth of successive 'ages', depicted in Poma de Ayala's* Nueva Corónica, *c.1615.*

or deity who afterwards took an overarching position but left daily issues to lesser, local deities.

The Incas tracked the movements of the sun and moon and created two calendars: a solar ('day-time'), 365-day year and a lunar ('night-time'), 328-day year. They do not seem to have been overly concerned with the 37-day discrepancy, possibly due to the fact that Inca calendrical observations were not essentially for the purpose of timekeeping. More important was to determine the correct times for religious rituals and festivals, to mark the beginning of important agricultural tasks, and to worship the sun and moon as deities.

The rotation of the Milky Way was important, but only the Pleiades, possibly the Southern Cross, and the summer and winter solstices were especially noted. More importantly, the voids between the stars, called 'dark cloud constellations', were envisaged as beasts known on Earth, and named after adult and baby llamas, the fox, the partridge, the toad and the snake and other animals.

Left: Believing Lake Titicaca to be the origin of the world, including the sun and the moon, the Incas built a temple to Inti on the Island of the Sun in the lake, to which Inca emperors made annual pilgrimages.

PILGRIMAGE, ORACLES AND SHRINES

Religious power and the ascendancy of priests in Andean civilization is evident in the monumentality of religious architecture. Ceremonial centres of terraced platforms, temples and ritual courtyards were focuses for communities of the surrounding regions. With true urbanism, from *c.*500BC, cities were dominated by their central ceremonial precincts.

RELIGIOUS TRADITIONS
Construction of common elements in ceremonial centres suggests widespread similarities in belief. Archaeologists recognize several early 'religious traditions', two of which flourished in the late Preceramic and Initial periods: the Kotosh Religious Tradition and the Plazas Hundidas Tradition. Significant in each is the division of space into forms that reflected religious belief, and that classified space horizontally and vertically, and as open and closed.

No ceremonial centre, however, appears to be dominant, although U-shaped ceremonial centres did serve local regions. The association of platform mounds and sunken courts nevertheless suggests the early link between a celestial deity and an earth mother.

Below: The fanged jaguar deity was one of several major themes in Chavín religious ritual, featured here in bas-relief on stone at Chavín de Huántar.

CHAVÍN DE HUÁNTAR
This settlement, which appears to have been deliberately located between the highlands and the coast, with access to exotic materials from deserts and tropical forests as well as locally, emerged in the Early Horizon as a unifying centre.

It was not a residential city. Rather it perpetuated the U-shaped temple tradition. A restricted residential complex was sufficient only for priests and attendants, and a limited number of craftspeople to produce portable objects with Chavín Cult imagery.

Celestial and earth deity association is evident in the embracing of a sunken court between the arms of U-shaped platform mounds. The Old Temple enclosed a circular sunken court and the New Temple a rectangular one. Projecting back the known importance of earth and sky association in Inca creation mythology, the Lanzón Stela in the central chamber of the Old Temple provides a metaphor of transition from earth to sky in its perforation of the upper gallery floor. So, too, the pairing, skyward gaze and invertibility of the Tello Stone caymans, the eagle and hawk of the Black and White Portal columns, and the Raimondi Stela in the New Temple.

Above: As well as animal figures, Nazca geoglyphs depicted sacred plants, here a cactus, on the desert floor. It forms a continuous line that never crosses itself, to form a ritual pathway.

The widespread distribution of Chavín symbolism in the north and central Andes, even as far as Paracas in the southern coastal desert, strengthens the argument that it was the earliest Andean 'international' pilgrimage site. The enlargement of the temple to a size that could accommodate 1,500 people in its courtyards and plazas reveals a growing importance over several hundred years of existence.

PACHACAMAC
The idea of a truly international pilgrimage site, a 'cathedral' for Andean religious worship, is well attested archaeologically and in Spanish documents for Pachacamac on the central Peruvian coast. Established in the early first millennium AD, its platform mound and windowless temple housing a wooden Pachacamac idol soon became a destination for pilgrims throughout the Andes.

Right: The pilgrimage temple and cult at Pachacamac endured for more than a millennium, a longevity and sacredness that the Incas could not ignore, but rather honoured and joined by building additional temples, including the so-called Temple of the Virgins.

Spanish eyewitness accounts in 1534 record that the city thronged with pilgrims, whose dress showed them to have come from throughout the Inca Empire. Priests, nobles and pilgrims were admitted and given accommodation in the vast complex of courts and rooms surrounding the temple. To enter the lower plaza of the temple, the supplicant had to 'fast' for 20 days. To enter the upper plaza meant a year-long 'fast'. ('Fasting' in this context required abstinence from salt, chilli peppers and sexual intercourse.)

ORACLE AT PACHACAMAC

The Pachacamac idol was veiled and only priests were allowed into the temple room itself. Questions put to the Pachacamac oracle concerned the weather, harvests, health matters and warfare. A priest relayed the god's answers to the supplicant, followed by hefty demands for tribute and donations. So powerful was the oracle that failure to comply with his mandates was believed to bring earthquakes and other natural disasters. Tupac Yupanqui, eleventh Inca Emperor and conqueror of the region, was made to fast for 40 days before he was allowed to consult the god; and, like other pilgrims, he was allowed to do so only through a cult priest. Even the mighty Inca had to recognize the importance of Pachacamac!

Lesser cults and their priests from all over the Andes sought alliance with the cult. Branch shrines were established only if they could assign lands and produce sufficient food to support a Pachacamac priest on site. Allied shrines were considered the 'wives', 'children' or 'brothers and sisters' of the Pachacamac Cult.

TIWANAKU

The power and well-documented status and longevity of Pachacamac provides archaeologists with powerful arguments for interpreting other sites as pilgrimage cities and oracles. As well as Chavín de Huántar, the Titicaca Basin appears to have been the focus of an early cult called the Yaya-Mama (male-female) Tradition, one of whose ceremonial centres was Early Horizon Pukará, north of the lake.

The region was soon dominated by Tiwanaku, however, whose empire flourished in the Middle Horizon. The size and complexity of Tiwanaku's platforms, sacrificial burials, sunken courtyards and symbolic statuary clearly reveal it to have been another pilgrimage and cathedral city. Recent research shows that in addition to its Akapana, Kalasasaya and Semi-Subterranean Court complex in the city centre, the Pumapunku complex almost 1 km (½ mile) to the south-west served as both a ritual gateway into the sacred city and a ceremonial theatre for worshipping pilgrims.

Left: Tiwanaku, pilgrimage centre and religious capital of an empire, had several large, stone-built temples and sacred compounds, including the Pumapunku – ritual gateway to the sacred city.

123

SACRIFICE, SLAUGHTER AND RITUAL

Human and animal sacrifices played an important role in ancient Andean civilization. They were widespread and very ancient. Sacrificial rituals accompanied religious worship and were often an aftermath of warfare, presumably also with religious motives.

The earliest example of human sacrifice is from late Preceramic Period Aspero. At the summit of the Huaca de los Sacrificios platform there were two burials, apparently dedicatory offerings to the gods to inaugurate the temple. One was an infant, specially adorned in a cap of 500 shell, plant and clay beads,

Below: On a Moche effigy stirrup-spouted red-line painted bottle, a transformed skeletal priest sacrifices a deer.

accompanied by a gourd vessel, wrapped in layers of cotton cloth and a cane mat and placed in a basket, then covered by a sculptured four-legged stone basin. The second was a sacrificed adult, whose body was so tightly flexed that that limbs had had to be cut to force the body into a small pit.

HUMAN SLAUGHTER

The great wall of carved stone slabs at Cerro Sechín is an early example of war-related sacrifice. Stacks of smaller slabs between tall slabs depicting triumphant warriors are carved with mutilated, contorted victims. The wall appears to be a war memorial. Agonized victims are shown nude, their torsos sliced with incised slashes, their eyes bulging with pain. Some bodies are headless, others limbless, some upside down. Blood and entrails spill out. There are disembodied legs, arms, rows of eyes, stacked vertebrae and heads with closed eyes. One victorious warrior carries a severed head dangling from his waistband.

Parallel themes occur on north coastal Cupisnique stone vessels and pottery. Carved steatite (soapstone) bowls depict spiders with exaggerated pincers, surrounded by severed heads. Ceramic effigy vessels show captives with bound hands, and stirrup-spout bottles are incised with severed heads, linked by cords or in net bags.

Farther north, at the late Valdivian Real Alto site, a stone-lined tomb on the summit of the low platform called the Charnal Mound contained a female burial. Next to the tomb was a dismembered male sacrificial victim surrounded by seven chert knives. Seven other male skeletons were in a common grave near by.

Two of the three high-relief adobe sculptures at Moxeke are of headless torsos, probably deliberately

Above: A principal Moche deity, and ritual sacrificer, imitated by priests was the Fanged God, depicted here in polychrome murals at the Huaca de la Luna at the Moche capital. He holds a sacrificial copper blade in his left hand.

decapitated, and the third is a colossal head, also probably a decapitation. The latest temple at Kotosh, towards the end of the Initial Period, included three headless bodies beneath the floor, presumably ritually decapitated to dedicate the temple.

SEVERED HEADS AND SACRIFICES

The tradition of severed heads was widespread and long-lived. Following these Initial Period examples, Early Horizon examples include more than 40 stone heads with tenons for mounting on the wall of the New Temple façade at highland Chavín de Huántar.

Within the central chamber of the Old Temple, the top of the Lanzón Stela comprises a spike from the deity's head, leaving a flat surface on top of the head. A groove carved from the tip of the spike down to the flat surface becomes shaped like a cross with a central depression, mirroring the plan of the Lanzón Gallery and the circular plaza. It is thought that blood from sacrificial victims was poured down the groove into the cross, eventually spilling over the stone itself. An engraved human finger bone was found in the gallery above the Lanzón.

Above: Ritual decapitation, probably combined in warfare and religious belief, began in the pre-Chavín Initial Period, as shown here by a warrior and decapitated victim on one of the temple wall slabs at Cerro Sechín.

In Paracas and Nazca on the south Peruvian coast, many burials include decapitated skulls and mutilated bodies, often with a cord around the neck or perforations in the skull meant for stringing them on a cord as a collection of trophy heads. Severed heads also adorn many Paracas and Nazca ceramics and textiles, especially in association with the Oculate Being – a flying deity figure shown trailing severed heads on streamers. Many Paracas and Nazca textiles are bordered with miniature woven severed heads.

THE MOCHE DECAPITATOR

Decapitator deities and imagery are known throughout Andean civilization.

Some of the most dramatic evidence of human sacrifice is that from the Moche. From the walls of Platform 1 of the Great Plaza of the Huaca de la Luna stares the grim face of the Decapitator God, with glaring white eyes, black hair and beard, and snarling mouth containing both human teeth and feline fangs. On Moche artefacts throughout the northern kingdom – ceramics, metalwork and textiles as well as architectural decoration – the Decapitator reminded Moche citizens daily of his grim presence.

As well as his face, he was depicted full-figured, holding a crescent-shaped *tumi* (ceremonial knife) and a severed human head. Intricate metalwork also shows spiders brandishing *tumi* knives and severed heads.

At Cao Viejo–El Brujo, the top terrace of a platform mound shows the segmented legs of a spider or crab Decapitator God brandishing a *tumi* sacrificial knife. (Before its destruction by looters, its fanged mouth was also visible.) Such imagery harks back to Cupisnique depictions in the same region.

SACRIFICE RITUAL

The Sacrifice Ritual depicted in Moche murals and in fine-line drawings on pottery involves four principal protagonists: the Warrior Priest, the Bird Priest, a Priestess and a feline-masked figure wearing a headdress with long, jagged-ended streamers. The ritual scene includes figures slitting the throats of naked sacrificial victims, then presenting the priests with goblets filled with the victims' blood. The now-destroyed Moche murals at Pañamarca showed the Priestess leading such a presentation procession: she carries a goblet and is followed by smaller figures presenting goblets and by a crawling, fanged serpent.

Moche sacrifice was intimately related to ritual combat. Warriors in Moche armour are depicted on pottery and as effigy vessels, pitted in single combat. The scenery appears to be the

Right: Sacred mountains were scenes of ritual sacrifice right up to Inca times. Here a Moche potter has depicted a ritual sacrifice on a mountain-shaped spouted bottle.

margins of fields. Successive scenes show the losing warrior stripped naked and with a rope around his neck, to be led away for sacrifice.

THE DECAPITATOR

Equally prominent among southern cultures was the Decapitator. Nazca portrayal of the Oculate Being with streaming severed heads has been mentioned. In the Pukará culture of the Titicaca Basin and its successor, Tiwanaku, the Decapitator and severed heads feature incessantly in stone sculpture, on pottery and textiles, in metalwork, and in wood and bone carving.

Scores of carved stone severed heads are mounted on

At San José Moro were found two graves with women buried in them. Both women wore and were accompanied by items identifying them as representatives of the Priestess in the mural at Pañamarca.

MASS GRAVES

Discoveries behind Moche's Huaca de la Luna platform, at Tiwanaku's Akapana platform and at Late Intermediate Period Batán Grande exemplify scenes of mass sacrifice that are reminiscent of the victory mutilations at Cerro Sechín.

At Moche an enclosure contained a mass grave of 40 men, aged 15 to 30. They appear to have been pushed into the grave from a stone outcrop after having been mutilated, then killed. Skulls,

Below: A Moche effigy jug in the form of a priest, partly transformed with feline fanged mouth and drug-glazed eyes, sacrificing two animals symbolic of Andean religious belief – a bird and a snake.

the walls of the Semi-Subterranean Courtyard. A special group of Tiwanaku stone sculptures known as *chachapumas* are puma-headed warriors holding a severed head and *tumi* knife.

Cut and polished human skulls found at Tiwanaku are evidence of the taking of trophy heads in battle – an Inca practice documented by Spanish chroniclers. (Inca warriors celebrated victory using drinking cups made from the skulls of important vanquished leaders.)

UNLOOTED TOMBS

Direct evidence of the reality of Moche sacrificial scenes was found in unlooted tombs discovered at Sipán in the Lambayeque Valley (dated *c.*AD300) and at San José Moro in the Jequetepeque Valley (*c.*AD600), showing that the practice was both widespread and of long duration. One Sipán tomb contained the burial of a figure that was dressed and

Above: The so-called prison quarter at Machu Picchu features a tomb-like cavern and sacrificial stone block carved as a condor (foreground).

accompanied by regalia identical to that of the Warrior Priest: back-flap, crescent-shaped rattles, ear-spools, a gold, crescent-shaped headdress, two *tumi* knives and a gold sceptre.

Not far from his tomb, a second tomb contained a body wearing an owl-adorned headdress, with grave goods, including a copper goblet and other items identifying him as the Bird Priest. Approximately 10m (33ft) west of the Bird Priest's tomb were sealed chambers filled with hundreds of pots, miniature copper war clubs, shields, headdresses and goblets. Scattered among these offerings were the skeletal remains of severed human hands and feet – presumably collected from sacrificial victims and stored.

Above: The Early Intermediate Period Nazca continued a long-practised tradition of ritual beheading, shown on this brightly painted bridge-spout bottle of a warrior holding his trophy head.

ribs and finger, arm and leg bones show cut marks. Some skeletons were splayed out as if tied to stakes; some had their femurs torn from the pelvis; and several skulls had their jaws torn away. The thick layer of rain-deposited sediment that covered the grave suggests that the sacrifice was performed in response to an El Niño weather event that disrupted the kingdom's economic stability, and that the offering was made to supplicate the wrath of the gods.

On the north-west corner of the first terrace of the Tiwanaku Akapana platform, excavators found 21 human burials mingled with llama bones and elegant pottery (dated c.AD600–800). Cut marks and compression fractures on the human bones reveal hacking with knives

and heavy blows from clubs. Some skeletons had selected bones removed; other burials were only of skulls or torsos. Many belonged to adult males aged 17–30; others were children.

Another Akapana 'burial' (dated c.AD600) was a destroyed chamber containing deliberately smashed pots, over which were splayed the skeleton of an adult male and the skull fragments of a juvenile. It has been suggested that these Akapana burials were sacrifices associated with a single momentous event, such as the dedication of the temple.

At the Sicán-Lambayeque city of Batán Grande, another mass grave contained 17 sacrificial victims accompanied by Ecuadorian conch shells, lapis lazuli, precious metal artefacts and 500kg (1,200lb) of copper artefacts.

CAPACOCHAS

Almost all Inca rituals included sacrifice, usually of llamas or guinea pigs. Brown llamas were sacrificed to Viracocha (the Creator), white to Inti (the Sun God) and dappled to Illapa (the Thunder). Animal sacrifices were performed by throat-slitting.

Coronations, war and natural catastrophes involved human sacrifice to solicit or supplicate the gods. The victims were provincial (non-Inca) children aged 10–15 years old. They needed to be physically perfect. After the victim had

Right: The ritual sacrifice of a black llama, depicted in Poma de Ayala's Nueva Corónica, c.1615.

been feasted, so as to offer him or her to Viracocha well satisfied, he/she was clubbed or strangled, and had the throat slit or the heart cut out and offered to Viracocha still beating.

A special child sacrifice – the *capacocha* – was preceded by a ritual procession along a straight sacred *ceque* line in Cuzco. The child's parents participated and considered the choice of their child to be an honour. *Capacocha* victims were sanctified in the Coricancha temple in Cuzco before walking back to be sacrificed in their province.

All of the ancient Andean cultures worshipped mountain gods. Only the Incas, however, ventured onto high peaks to kill and bury sacrificial victims there. Special sacrifices were made of children, who were marched barefoot to the mountain-top, where they were clubbed or strangled – or even buried alive – and interred with miniature dressed human figurines, miniature gold or silver llama figurines, and pouches containing their baby teeth and nail parings. Such sacrifices have been discovered on Cerro el Pomo and Mount Acongagua in northern Chile, and on Ampato in Peru and Llullaillaco in northern Argentina.

INDEX